First Aid for Meetings

Quick Fixes and Major Repairs
for Running Effective Meetings

Charlie Hawkins

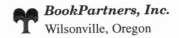

BookPartners, Inc.
Wilsonville, Oregon

BookPartners, Inc.

P.O. Box 922
Wilsonville, Oregon 97070

Acknowledgments

The strategies, ideas and techniques in *First Aid for Meetings* have evolved over almost three decades of attending, leading, facilitating and arranging meetings of all kinds. In a sense, every meeting in which I have been involved has provided a contribution to this work — the great ones, the disasters and those in between.

Stating an intention is one thing; like many, I have long wanted to write a worthwhile book sharing what I have learned. Getting a start was relatively easy; I have "started" many books over the years, even if some of them never made it past the title and first few pages. Following through and completing the manuscript required a focus and discipline not common to my frenzied (and wonderful) life of facilitating, consulting and speaking.

Alicia, my wife and best friend, was my main encourager throughout the process. Her gentle reminders to make time to write enabled me to keep the book going in the midst of many other priorities. She also read every chapter, providing wise counsel and helpful editing comments.

Meeting Thorn and Ursula Bacon of BookPartners was a turning point. After one delightful meeting, they encouraged me to turn my dream into a reality. Since then, working with them through the entire process has been delightful — quite different from the stereotyped image of the publishing business I had imagined.

Chris Hauri gave me a vision for the structure over dinner one night. As colleagues for ten years, we have endured the best and worst of times in meetings. Many of the ideas for the section on telephone/video meetings came from Paul Burgess and Lorraine Parker.

Jennifer Cowan, Al Croft, Chuck Fuhrman, Grace Hawkins, Jack Llewellyn, Bob Savard and Chris Suffolk each read various portions (and versions) of the manuscript and provided invaluable comments. Thanks to you all.

Table of Contents

Introduction

"Let's have a meeting."

If those familiar words make you shudder, you are not alone. Meetings are renowned as time-wasters and bores, and it is a wonder that anything at all gets accomplished at certain meetings. It seems that few organizations are immune: companies of all sizes, associations, professional groups, government, academic institutions, hospitals, churches, volunteer organizations and clubs center many of their activities around meetings. *Business Week* estimates that over eleven million meetings are held in the U.S. every business day. Other studies show that managers spend from 30 percent to a whopping 70 percent of their time every day in meetings.

When meetings are effective, the potential for results is unlimited. Things get done. Participants feel energized and valued. They contribute freely, find solutions, and make decisions. A "live" meeting is the only place where people can communicate with their eyes, voice and body language in a dynamic interchange of ideas and opinions. Even though we are able to communicate electronically via phones, satellites or computers, it's simply not the same as a face-to-face meeting.

Yet many — if not most — meetings are "sick" in some way. Some are tedious and boring, seldom staying focused. Many people confide that they are reluctant to volunteer for committees, simply because the meetings are so long and tiresome. Some groups follow the same routine meeting after meeting, seemingly going nowhere and accomplishing nothing. Most of us rightly consider meetings a monumental waste of time. Still other meetings leave people "wounded" or manipulated in some way, because the leader or other participants discount or squash their ideas. Perhaps they are victims of hidden agendas. After such meetings, people leave feeling drained and often angry.

" Things were fine, until we started having meetings."

It seems that more of us should be able to "get it right," because meetings have an enormous potential for effective collaboration. I suspect that most people would like to change the way they "do" meetings but don't know how. Is there any hope? Yes! After planning, facilitating, observing and participating in thousands of meetings during twenty-eight years of a business and counseling career, I have seen dramatic improvement in meetings when participants learn and practice a few basic skills. Even more encouraging is the news that anyone — and any group — can learn and practice these techniques.

This book is not a prescription or a rigid model for meetings, neither does it suggest that there is only one "right way" to run meetings. In fact, there are many right ways to run meetings. However, prescriptions in *First Aid for Meetings* will point you in the right direction and show you how even small changes can make a big difference in any meeting you run or attend. As you try a few of the antidotes and techniques, and experiment with others, you'll gradually develop some healthy options for your organization's meetings. Who knows, you might even grow to look forward to meetings!

Who Should Read This Book?

Anyone who leads, facilitates, presents or participates in small group meetings (from two to twenty-five people) can benefit from the tools and ideas in *First Aid for Meetings*. While many of the techniques also apply to larger groups, this book concentrates on the small- to medium-sized meetings that are the norm for most organizations.

I once thought that business meetings were different from meetings in other groups, such as schools and colleges, churches, clubs and volunteer organizations. In many respects they differ, especially when group members are volunteers rather than employees. Over the years, however, I've learned that there are more similarities than differences. People are people. After all, many of the same people who meet in volunteer groups also participate in business meetings.

Thus, these prescriptions for effective meetings work in any type of organization. If you belong to one of these groups, you will find something of value in these pages.

Medium and Large Business Organizations

Directors, executives, managers, department heads, team leaders, committee or subcommittee heads, internal consultants, supervisors, trainers, administrative assistants, meeting planners, team members, task force and committee members.

Small Businesses

Owners, executives, managers, supervisors, team leaders and all employees who plan, lead, facilitate or attend meetings.

Volunteer and Non-Profit Groups

Executives, staff, full-time or part-time trainers, committee heads, board members, volunteers who attend trainings or other meetings.

Hospitals and Health Care Facilities

Chiefs of staff, administrators, board members, department heads, chief/attending surgeons, residents, supervisors, nurses, staff personnel, committee members.

Academic Institutions

Superintendents, school board members, principals, deans, administrators, departments, professors, teachers, instructors, counselors, staff support, PTA leaders.

Consultants

Trainers, planners, strategists, conference facilitators, subject matter experts, general or specialized consultants.

Professionals and Professional Associations

Doctors, lawyers, accountants, architects, consulting engineers, and staff support personnel.

Churches/Religious Institutions

Clergy, staff, board chairs, officers and members, deacons, committee leaders and members, administrators.

Clubs and Associations

Officers, committee members and chairs, staff support people, program planners, and members who plan or attend meetings.

Part I

Before the Meeting:
The Four P's of Planning

Before the Meeting:
The Four P's of Planning

1. Purpose

Establish and communicate the reason(s) you are meeting. Determine if a meeting is really necessary.

2. People

Decide on the people who will attend based on whether they can help achieve the purpose. Clarify the roles of each participant.

3. Place

Select the right location, meeting space, and room setup to accomplish your purpose.

4. Preparation

Select the most important items to be discussed, solved or decided and write an agenda; then plan the process, give participants advance materials, and handle logistics arrangements.

1

Purpose

The truth you never hear:

"Well, uh, it's about ten after, so let's go ahead and start the meeting. As usual, we're, um, not really sure why we're getting together, except that, well, we always meet on Mondays. Oh, I think Sam's got something to report on the southern region. Anytime you think of something, speak up, even if it is off the subject, and you interrupt someone else. Uh, we'll keep going until we run out of steam, and we'll all probably be frustrated when we end, because we will have accomplished very little."

The Symptoms:

No Purpose Defined or Unclear Purpose

When the purpose of a meeting is not defined or is unclear, people often find themselves in the midst of a discussion that is irrelevant to them. Without a purpose, meetings flounder, turning into a forum for discussing anything that pops into participants' minds. Starting a meeting without a purpose is like beginning a trip without a specific destination in mind. If it is not clear why the group has been called together, few participants will know how to prepare. Without a stated purpose, the meeting may start with vague comments and wander in several different directions before finally ending. Often, little gets accomplished, and participants are frustrated at having wasted so much time with nothing to show for it.

The Trap of Regularly Scheduled Meetings

Regularly scheduled meetings are often guilty of not having a definite purpose. Almost every organization where I have been associated has held daily, weekly or monthly staff meetings. These meetings occur at the executive level, in most mid-level departments, and at the operating level. Often staff and committee meetings become institutionalized, then continue to be called whether or not they are really necessary. While regularly scheduled meetings tend to follow a set format (e.g., each department head reports, old business/new business, etc.), the purpose of these meetings is seldom questioned, or even known.

Paragon Cleaning Products was a successful, medium-sized industrial cleaning products company. Every Wednesday without fail, the eleven-member staff attended a luncheon meeting at a nearby restaurant. Each staff member was expected to have something prepared to present to the other members.

There was no set format for the presentations. Seth, the head of operations, usually recited a laundry list of problems his department was experiencing, in a whining tone of voice. Joe, the controller, talked about deals going down and the status of the financial markets — Joe always brought along a couple of charts. Agnes, who ran the marketing department, often talked about new campaigns about to break, or other activities such as market research. Woody, the head of international sales, usually shared some outrageous story about taking a thirty-six-hour trip to Nairobi for a two-hour meeting.

And so it went. The food was good, the camaraderie was great, and nothing was ever discussed that made much of a difference. The meetings started at noon and seldom finished before two o'clock, often running much longer. The president never fixed a purpose for these luncheons, and no one on the operating committee seemed to know the reason for the meetings. It seemed as if the main purpose was social. If so, many people wasted a lot of hours preparing presentations of little interest to anyone else. Important decisions of Paragon Cleaning Products were seldom made at the weekly meetings.

First Aid for Aimless Meetings:

- Determine as precisely as possible the purpose(s) of the meeting.
- Decide whether a meeting is really necessary; understand when other alternatives may work better.
- Communicate the purpose of the meeting to all who are invited to attend.

- As a participant, ask the leader if the purpose of a meeting has not been clearly communicated.
- Avoid ulterior purposes.

Determine the Purpose(s) of the Meeting:

The starting point to determine the purpose is to ask yourself what you expect to accomplish. What should the participants think, feel or accomplish as a result of the meeting? Below are some of the more common purposes for meetings:

Give and receive information such as announcements, results, status reports, committee reports, and presentations on subjects of interest to participants.

- Staff meetings, committee meetings
- Project status reports and updates
- Sales meetings
- Marketing and sales presentations

Coordinate projects, calendars and assignments.

- Department heads or committee meetings
- Team meetings

Learning or study — skills, procedures or operations.

- Training meetings and seminars
- New employee orientation meetings
- Team training
- Professional organizations, club meetings, and study groups

Planning — establish a vision, set goals, determine objectives, and develop strategies.

- Board, team or departmental retreats
- Cross-functional team meetings
- Newly formed groups
- Planning for major presentations or events

Solve problems — analyze issues, generate ideas and possible solutions, create opportunities.

- Ad-hoc groups or task forces formed to address specific situations such as employee absenteeism, or generate funds for a new building
- Functional teams
- Committees, boards, departmental groups

Make decisions — evaluate and rank alternatives, select and prioritize options, reach consensus, assign action steps.

- Groups that meet to generate ideas or solve problems
- Any group that is presented with alternatives developed by others

Socialize — get to know one another, and network.

- Groups primarily designed to foster networking, such as clubs and associations
- Often a valuable component of meetings called for other purposes

Build teamwork — create trust, inspire, motivate and celebrate success.

- A useful purpose for teams or groups that are forming
- Meetings to announce and celebrate successful results or high achievers

From this list, it may be obvious that many meetings have more than one purpose; for example, sometimes it's useful to generate ideas and then make decisions. Task force or team meetings might include building teamwork as an ongoing objective, even if it's not a defined purpose at any single meeting. Being clear about the purpose is the foundation for all other aspects that contribute to an effective meeting.

Decide if the Meeting is Necessary

Many meetings are held out of habit or impulse — the "we always meet on Wednesday morning" syndrome. The least productive meetings are ones where the goals can be accomplished in another less-costly and time-consuming way. Here are some questions to ask to discover if a meeting is really necessary:

- What would be gained or lost if the meeting were not held?
- Can the same aims be accomplished by memo, fax, mail, or e-mail?
- Can a series of one-on-one discussions be held to accomplish the same goal in less time?

- If you hold regular staff or committee meetings, consider scheduling half as many meetings, such as every other week or month. Use phone messages or mail to communicate between meetings.

Other reasons for not holding a meeting:

- When there is not enough time for participants to prepare.
- When your mind is already made up, and you really do not want input or ideas.
- When the subject is confidential.

Communicate the Purpose
to Everyone Attending

There are few things more disconcerting than being invited to a meeting without being informed what it is all about. At the very least, you feel unprepared. In the absence of information, many of us assume the worst — we start thinking our department is being eliminated or something else equally disastrous.

Of course, there are times when confidentiality or sensitivity dictates that the purpose not be announced in advance. But most of the time, a little prior information is useful. As the leader, it is to your advantage to have people join your meeting with an informed point of view. How will they be able to prepare and fully participate if they don't know what the purpose is?

Ask the Leader

If you are invited to a meeting and the purpose is not clear, simply ask the leader (or other person who calls it) or his/her assistant. This does not have to be a confrontation, simply a request. Knowing the purpose will enable you to prepare in advance, and to determine whether or not it is worth your time to attend, if you have a choice.

Avoid Ulterior Purposes

Ulterior purposes are a little trickier; you might also call them hidden agendas. This happens when you are told you are meeting for one purpose, but there is something else entirely different going on, usually quite subtle.

The members of the fund-raising committee for a community volunteer group were frequently asked for ideas. As ideas were offered from the members, Evelyn, the chair, frequently responded with killer phrases such as, "We'll never get that past the board" and "we tried something like that three years ago and it didn't work."

On the other hand, Evelyn would often present her ideas and promote them enthusiastically. To be fair, some of them were pretty good. The problem was that the only ideas she supported were her own. It wasn't too long before ideas from the rest of the committee members dried up. Then Evelyn began to complain that she was the only one who came up with ideas.

It became clear that Evelyn's ulterior purpose, whether she was aware of it or not, was to elicit the group's reactions to her ideas. The committee fell apart after several months, with most members feeling unappreciated and manipulated. Evelyn complained about how hard it was to get volunteers to serve on committees, never suspecting she may have been part of the problem.

As a meeting leader, the best way to avoid ulterior purposes is to honestly examine what you really want to accomplish, and to let everyone know. If you simply want to get reactions to your ideas, just say so. Having established this purpose, you also need to set the climate for honest evaluation and feedback. If all you want is positive feedback, why hold a meeting? Few things diminish group members more than to be told their ideas are wanted, only to have them systematically judged or dismissed by a meeting leader who really does not want input from others. Sadly, leaders are not always aware of what they are doing.

As a participant, you may be able to pick up ulterior motives by comparing what the leader says to what he or she actually does. If the ideas of you and other participants are not valued, there is probably an ulterior motive to the meeting. Unfortunately, there is little you can do in most situations, except to find a reason to skip the next meeting.

Another ulterior purpose of some meetings is to evaluate people, especially when a manager or supervisor is convening with subordinates. Then the meeting becomes a showcase to see how the employees perform under pressure. Certainly, anyone who makes a presentation to a group is under pressure, especially if they are new at it. More subtly, people are also evaluated according to their contributions. Whether meeting leaders acknowledge it or not, the fact remains that meetings are a visible forum for many people. In some cases, it may be the only time a leader sees an employee or member "in action."

The best solution to this situation is for the leader to also get to know people outside the meeting environment, thus developing a more well-rounded view of how they perform in different situations. Similarly, participants should seek chances to meet with the leader one-on-one and in other situations, so that the staff meeting is not their only exposure.

2

People

The truth you never hear:

"I have called the entire staff together, even though most of you won't have a chance to participate, and are not really affected in the slightest way by most of the things we will be discussing or deciding."

The Symptoms:

Participants Not Involved

Has this ever happened to you? You're sitting in a meeting wondering why in the world you are there. While the subject is marginally relevant to you, it is something you could easily read in a memo or meeting summary. As the meeting progresses, you "zone out," resorting to doodling on your notepad and imagining all the better things you could be doing rather than wasting time in the meeting.

When Carolyn Fisher was a Major in the U.S. Air Force, she often attended Department of Defense meetings about upcoming plans for politically sensitive programs. Over time, she noticed that many people who might be involved with these programs at later stages would also attend the early planning meetings "to see what was happening." As a result, the meetings often bogged down with questions from people whose involvement was not critical in the planning stage. The meetings ultimately became difficult to manage because of sheer numbers.

Key People Absent

The opposite situation occurs when topics of interest to certain people are discussed, and they are not present. Maybe they are on vacation or a business trip, and perhaps the topics surfaced because of issues in other areas. Or maybe the leader just forgot to invite them. Whatever the reason, things can really get fouled up quickly if people who have a stake in a discussion or decision are not included.

Roles Not Assigned

Other symptoms of ineffective meetings show up when clear roles have not been assigned to make the meeting run smoothly. As a result, the meeting may easily teeter off-course, time is not managed well, and ultimately the purpose is not accomplished.

First Aid for Participation

- Trim the attendee list to the absolute minimum number of people; make sure only the necessary people attend.

- Consider having part-time participants.
- If you are invited to a meeting which you feel is of only marginal interest to you or not the best use of your time, ask the leader if your presence is mandatory. If you choose to stay, use the meeting as a learning opportunity.
- Assign key roles to make the meeting run smoothly.

Trim the Attendee List to the Absolute Minimum — Invite the Right People

Assess the value of each participant in helping fulfill the purpose you have set for the meeting. Is the entire staff required? Do all the committee members need to attend every meeting? Consider inviting a team (committee, department) representative rather than having an entire group attend.

Who Should Attend a Meeting?

- People who can influence or help accomplish the meeting's purpose.
- People who have a stake in the subjects covered, especially those who will be affected by decisions made. It is perfectly legitimate to invite people whose attendance would further your purpose, such as getting a recommendation "sold" to higher or different levels.
- People who have information to share, like subject matter experts and people making or participating in presentations.

- People who can make positive contributions, like problem-solvers, idea generators, astute observers, and experts in the subject area.
- People to observe the meeting for training or consultation purposes. Be careful to limit the number of "outsiders" attending for this reason.

Consider Carefully Before Inviting:

- People who cannot or are not willing to contribute to accomplishing the meeting's purpose.
- People who are prone to display disruptive behavior in meetings. Chapter 13 lists many of these behaviors and how to deal with them. The best way to deal with disruptive people is to not invite them in the first place!
- People who have only a peripheral interest in the subject(s) being covered. If necessary, send people in this category a copy of the meeting notes or debrief them separately.
- People whose title or temperament would result in them feeling "hurt" if they weren't invited but have no other valid reason for attending.

Consider Rescheduling Your Meeting If:

- People who are critical to the issue being discussed or decision being made are not able to attend, and their contribution or influence would make a difference in the outcome. At the very least, consider including them via phone or video conference.

- Members do not have enough time to prepare properly.

Is there an ideal number of people who should attend a meeting? As a general guideline, the fewer the better. If there is to be any meaningful interaction and involvement, a group size of less than ten is preferable. Five to eight people is a great group size for generating ideas and making decisions.

When Major Carolyn Fisher became the leader for project planning meetings, she developed a list of people who were critical to the project at the first stage. It turned out to be about half the number who had previously attended. Those not on the list were simply not invited, and if they showed up anyway (some persisted!) they were politely asked to leave.
The results were immediate. The planning meetings were more highly focused, and more was accomplished in less time. When projects moved into the final stages, Major Fisher invited those who were affected to briefing meetings.

Larger groups work well when the communication is essentially one way. For example, when a general announcement must be made, and it is important that everyone hears it at the same time from the same person, a large group get-together works fine. Also, celebrations, recognition events, and keynote speeches are effective in large group settings. Even in these settings, it is often a good idea to break the large group into smaller sub-groups for discussion, idea-generation and feedback.

Consider running pre-meetings with a group of participants who are a sub-set of a larger group. One volunteer board I belong to holds executive meetings midway between regular monthly meetings to review issues and make decisions that don't require the attention of the full twenty-member board. The result is that the regular board meetings have been shortened from several hours to an average of an hour and a half.

Consider Having Part-time Attendees

It is not always necessary for everyone involved to attend the entire meeting. One method is to first meet with the entire group for a discussion of items of general interest. After the general issues are covered, everyone except those who are directly affected by the remaining specific items is free to leave.

At a chemical plant in Texas, twelve maintenance department supervisors convened every morning for about an hour. Even though their purpose was to coordinate crews and schedules, the meetings were not highly structured, nor were they productive. In fact, the most frequent agenda item was, "Who brought the donuts?" Because the group met every day, there was a lot of kidding around and socializing.

Juanita, the manager in charge, estimated the cost of the daily meetings by calculating an hourly equivalent of the salaries and benefits of everyone attending. The result was a raw meeting cost of $485 per hour. This translated to $2,425 a week for five meetings and $121,250 a year, if the meetings averaged an hour in length. And this was just one work group!

Then she asked participants to "guesstimate" what they could be doing with their time if they were not involved in the daily meetings, and to put a price to their time. While this "opportunity cost" was more difficult to calculate, it was estimated to be at least as high as the salary cost for time squandered in meetings.

As a result of this analysis, Juanita cut the meetings to once a week and had the entire group attend for only a half-hour. If any supervisors had problems or specific issues to discuss, those who were involved stayed on. The rest of the business of the group was conducted via e-mail and one-on-one meetings.

Uninvite Yourself if the Meeting Is Not Relevant to You

This bold move may be tricky if your boss is the person calling the meeting. However, you may be applauded for astutely managing your priorities. One way to approach this is to explain to the leader what other items are on your "hot" list which you believe are more important than spending time in a meeting of marginal relevance.

Of course, the leader may have reasons to invite you that he or she doesn't make clear at first. Your request to skip the meeting may prompt more candid communications about the purpose. Maybe your objective point of view is needed. Sometimes it is productive to have a marketing person assess a manufacturing issue or a volunteer coordinator review the budget. Then there's the possibility that the leader may agree with your assessment and excuse you from attending.

As the new minister of a Presbyterian church in central Arizona, Arnie was invited to attend every meeting held by every committee in the church. At first, Arnie thought this was useful, because it gave him a good understanding of what each group did, and it was a good way to get to know some of the more active members.

Then Arnie began to realize the committee chairs wanted more than his attendance. They wanted him to make or "bless" major decisions, which is the way they functioned with the former minister. Since Arnie preferred to let the committees decide things on their own, he began to tactfully "uninvite" himself from the meetings.

At first, the committee chairs thought Arnie didn't care and resented his absence. Over time, however, they realized how much more enthusiastic committee members felt when they were empowered to decide things on their own. Of course, Arnie was brought into critical situations when it was necessary, but he learned about each committee's routine work at the monthly session meetings.

Use the Meeting as a Learning Opportunity

If you find yourself trapped in a meeting that isn't relevant or important to you, ask to leave if possible. If there is no way out, why not use the occasion to observe the process and learn something. For example, focus on what makes the meeting effective or not effective — what is the meeting leader or facilitator doing that makes the meeting work well? Who is participating and who is not? If you are an "outsider," you might discover that your detachment from the subject gives you clarity and the ability to contribute useful ideas and suggestions.

Assign Key Roles
to Make the Meeting Function Smoothly

In the typical small group meeting, there are only two roles identified: the leader and everybody else! Sometimes a recorder is appointed, often accompanied by groans of, "Do I have to?" However, meetings can take quantum leaps if people are assigned key roles and perform the functions of those roles. These include:

The leader is the person who calls the meeting, decides who attends, and sets the tone. The leader is often the elected or appointed head of a group, such as the manager, chair, committee head, or team leader.

The facilitator plans and runs the meeting, keeps things on track, keeps people involved and remains neutral on issues.

The recorder takes notes without editing or evaluating during the meeting and distributes a summary afterwards.

The timekeeper keeps track of time and signals the facilitator and the group at appropriate points during the meeting.

Participants are members who prepare properly, receive and share information and ideas, analyze issues, and generally contribute to achieving the meeting purpose.

Resource people prepare and present information, answer questions, and contribute advice of a general or specific nature.

It may seem like overkill to have all these roles in a meeting of only a few people. It's not. With these roles clearly identified and performed satisfactorily, your meeting can become more effective. You'll get more things done in less time and keep everyone involved and interested throughout.

For many functions, people can serve in more than one role, but there is one major trap to avoid. Most groups get in trouble by combining the roles of leader and facilitator. Why? Because the leader is often the most powerful person in the meeting because of his/her title or authority, and usually has strong points of view on the issues discussed. After all, the leader calls the meeting, which by itself carries a level of influence or authority. By contrast, the facilitator is charged with running the meeting process. As a result, he or she must be impartial and neutral on issues and ideas.

Many leaders do a good job of facilitating until an issue comes up where they have a strong opinion or vested interest. It is difficult to stay neutral when this happens.

> Sheila had training and experience facilitating idea-generating sessions. As a project group leader, she decided to facilitate brainstorming sessions for her group instead of turning it over to someone else. During the sessions, Sheila would often come up with ideas which she thought were pretty good. If she was not careful, she would catch herself not only offering ideas, but trying to persuade others of their value.
>
> Eventually Sheila discovered that this bias undermined her credibility both as a facilitator and as a project group leader. She learned the wisdom of bringing in a neutral facilitator for her group projects. She has also offered her services as a facilitator to teams in which she has no other involvement.

Some leaders may be uncomfortable having someone else run "their" meeting. This might be a control issue, or a perception that having a facilitator somehow diminishes their authority. If leaders are trained in facilitation skills —

some are — and can remain neutral throughout, then combining the two roles might work.

But even if it works, what's the benefit? Running an effective meeting is hard work, and it precludes leaders from fully participating. Taking the first step to separate the role of the leader from the role of the facilitator is a big one. The results are worth it.

It is sometimes possible and often practical to combine the roles of facilitator and recorder. The trade-off is that it slows down the meeting process. This important subject will come up again in Chapter 5.

Resource people quite often play multiple roles in meetings. The leader may present some information, and any participant may also be a resource person. Usually, the timekeeper's duties are handled by one of the participants.

For best results, the key meeting roles should be rotated. It helps if several people in a group are trained and prepared to facilitate. Most people can learn how to be an effective recorder without too much difficulty. Rotating these responsibilities keeps more people involved and helps educate members about group process, meeting dynamics, and time management.

The Function of Meeting Planners

Many organizations have full-time or part-time meeting planners, or use consulting groups or specialists to plan meetings. Because planners are used most often for larger, more complex meetings and events, this book does not address the planning functions as a separate role. If there is no designated meeting planner, the meeting preparation steps usually fall to the leader or facilitator or perhaps an administrative assistant.

If your organization is fortunate enough to have a meeting planner, he or she can assist considerably in making sure the planning and logistics are covered thoroughly. Meeting planners are trained to "sweat the small stuff," know the right questions to ask, and how to deal with hotels and conference facilities. To use meeting planners effectively, involve them in the early stages of planning and share as much information with them as possible.

3

Place

The Symptoms:

Room Inappropriate for Meeting

You are in a room that is clearly wrong for the meeting. It would hold a small army, yet there are only eight of you huddled in a lonely corner. The size of the room, along with its dark, massive furnishings, suggests an air of formality that hardly seems conducive for brainstorming new ideas. At the opposite extreme, there are fifteen of you squeezed into a room that comfortably holds six. Some people are forced to stand or otherwise deal with their discomfort throughout the meeting. Churches, schools, hospitals, community centers and other special-purpose buildings usually have excellent facilities for everything but small meetings. You know what this means if you have ever attended a finance committee meeting in a kindergarten classroom, or a training session in the corner of a gymnasium or dining area. Many meetings are held without a lot of thought given to the impact that the space will have on the meeting's purpose. For example, a meeting in the boss's office sets a different tone than meeting in a conference room.

Noise Distractions

If you hold a meeting in a hotel, you can almost bet there will be distracting noises from the banquet in the adjoining room or clatter emanating from the kitchen. By their very nature, hotel ballrooms and breakout rooms have to be flexible to accommodate a variety of meeting sizes and types. Unfortunately, this often results in sound leaks from one meeting to another, or from the kitchen. Other distractions can come from the loud ambient noise of heating or cooling systems, from workers cleaning the carpet in the next room, or from lawnmowers just outside your meeting room window. I have even been in meetings where the proceedings were accompanied by Muzak™ on the PA system.

Of course, noise distractions are not limited to hotel meeting rooms. The problem is that noise distractions divert the group's attention to the noise source, and some participants will not be able to hear the speakers.

Room Setup Not Conducive to Meeting's Purpose

When little thought is given to how chairs and other furnishings are arranged, subtle dynamics come into play which can affect a meeting. For example, in a session designed to generate ideas, a room arrangement that does not allow group members to interact easily with each other will not be as effective as one that does.

Why are the place and space so important? The room sets a tone for the meeting. If it is inviting, people will feel better and are likely to be better participants. If the meeting room is not right, it can drain the participants' energy and contribute to a less-effective meeting.

Two recent meetings I attended dramatize the impact of environment on the results. The purpose of each meeting was to generate ideas: one for new products and the second for merchandising concepts for a line of beverages.

As I walked into the room for the new products session, I could almost feel my energy draining. The room was drab and cluttered with boxes of materials; big, over-stuffed chairs were set up around a dark conference table. Because the chairs were so large, there was little room for anyone to move. The lighting was poor, and the walls were bare, except for a faded print that looked half a century old.

By contrast, the room we used for developing the merchandising concepts was bright and festive. Participants felt immediately energized when they entered the room. Two areas were set up within a larger space — one had tables and chairs and was used for presenting material and for voting to select the best concepts. The second area — where we generated ideas — held sofas and comfortable chairs, colorful decorations, product displays and sketches, plants and bright lighting. The promotion agency working on this project created these spaces, ultimately a stimulating environment.

While good ideas were generated in both sessions, it was an uphill battle in the new products group "overcoming" the room. There was no question that the environment in the merchandising session contributed to an output of creative ideas from the participants.

First Aid for Meeting Spaces

- Evaluate the size, location, furnishings, lighting and other dynamics in view of the purpose of the meeting. Select a space that will help participants focus on this purpose with as few distractions as possible.
- Hold meetings in "neutral territory."
- Arrange the room to help the group accomplish the meeting purpose.
- Recognize that other meetings will happen outside the regular meeting room.

Evaluate Size, Location, Furnishings and Other Dynamics

There are many factors related to the meeting location which can affect a group's productivity. This list will give you an idea of some of the things you should consider when choosing a meeting site.

Ideal size: Large enough for every participant to be comfortable, small enough for some degree of intimacy. Twelve people seated in an auditorium would feel overwhelmed by the room; twelve people in a typical office would be cramped.

- If the meeting purpose is to generate ideas, allow enough space for flip charts or other tools at the front of the room.
- If the room is too large, use plants or screens to section off the meeting area.

Ideal location: Convenient for all and easy to find. No one likes to be embarrassed by being late to a meeting because it is difficult to find.

- If you are at the office (church, hospital, school, community center), look for the room or rooms that are best suited for your meeting's purpose.
- Provide maps and written directions if there is any doubt about how to locate the building and the room. If you have ever arrived "on time" for a meeting, only to spend several minutes wandering around unfamiliar buildings looking for Conference Room 4 West A or some other mysterious code, you will appreciate this suggestion.

Ideal furnishings: Seating that is comfortable for an hour or more of sitting, but not too plush; tables for writing (if required); live plants and artwork to help set the tone.

- Avoid large conference tables if possible; they are not conducive to a give-and-take group environment.

- For a creative brainstorming session, toys, puzzles and games inspire playful and open-minded creativity.
- Try a meeting without a table or even without chairs — a stand-up meeting can be highly effective in some circumstances.

Ideal lighting: Bright, indirect lighting. Try to arrange for a room that has dimmers to control the intensity. Remember that lights may have to be dimmed if slides or computer visuals are shown.

Ideal heating and ventilation: Comfortable, with good circulation and the ability to adjust.

- Adjustable heating or cooling is a must; keep the room on the cooler side (68 to 70 degrees) at first, until the effect of body heat kicks in.

Ideal access: Close to bathrooms and break areas; access for any physically-challenged persons attending.

Ideal noise level: Low ambient noise, no major distractions, and no surprises.

At a planning workshop to create a long-term vision for a company, we came to consensus on a vision statement at the end of a long morning session. At the moment the final vision statement was written on a flip chart, we heard another group singing "God Bless America" in the adjacent room. Normally, having the Rotary Club luncheon meeting in the adjacent room would be distracting, but in this case it was momentous.

Hold the Meeting in Neutral Territory

A meeting that is held in someone's office usually gives him or her a subtle advantage. If it is the boss's office, it can be intimidating to others. For the best results, select a site for meeting which favors no one person or entity. A conference room is almost always a good choice. Why else do you suppose so many meetings involving world powers are held in neutral countries, like Switzerland?

If there is no other choice than to meet in an office, try to avoid having the boss sit behind a desk, which places a barrier between him or her and other participants. If there is enough room, set up chairs in a separate area of the office. Fortunately, many larger offices have a separate conference area — use it.

Arrange the Room to Help Accomplish the Purpose

If you want involvement — and why wouldn't you? — the best way to encourage it is to allow group members to see each other. The configurations that are best suited for easy discussions are circles, squares, semicircles, and U-shaped seating arrangements. Most other room setups force some people to look at the backs of heads.

Circles and squares (can be set up with or without a table)

- Advantages: Circles and squares encourage active participation from everyone; it is not easy to hide. Circles "equalize" participants and can increase intimacy if no tables are used.
- Drawbacks: They can be unwieldy for larger groups of fifteen or more. There is also no focal

point for presentations or "group notes." If ideas need to be written on flip charts, some members will have to break the circle to see. It is sometimes difficult to use audio/visual equipment effectively. Circles intensify the mood of the group; squares do this also, but to a lesser extent. Since energy is directed at other people, this set-up may be too intense for some meetings.

When to use circles: For groups of up to ten to twelve, especially for committee reporting, discussion and group idea-generation, "rounds" of six to ten people are a good setup for larger meetings where subgroups or breakouts will be formed for discussion, feedback and brainstorming.

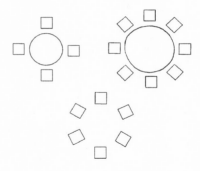

Ovals (Ovals are obviously similar to circles, usually with a conference table. Many conference rooms have a permanent oval table in them.)

- Advantages: Ovals have most of the same advantages as circles.
- Drawbacks: Participants sit facing another person across the table, which could be intense; yet, they are unable to connect with people sitting to their left or right. Participants in many meetings around

oval tables often "take sides," such as members from the marketing department sitting on one side of the table and operations on the other.

When to use ovals: When you don't have a choice. You will find ovals in conference rooms more often than not. Staff and committee meetings can work effectively in oval configurations, especially if the leader does not assume the head position at one end. Leave one end open for audio/visual equipment and presen-tations.

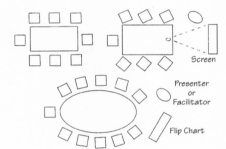

Semicircle (including U-shaped; usually with tables)

- Advantages: By placing audio/visual screens and flip chart easels at the open end, this provides a natural focal point on presenters, the facilitator, and the work of the group. It's easy to make eye contact and it promotes interactive participation. A semicircle is not as intense as a circle or square and allows the facilitator or presenters to move in and out of the "U."
- Drawbacks: This seating form can be unwieldy for large groups and may draw undue attention to the facilitator. Sometimes space limitations or fixed furniture in many meeting rooms make semicircles or U-shapes impractical.

When to use semicircles or U-shape: These arrangements work well for generating ideas, problem-solving, or any meeting where lots of participation is desired.

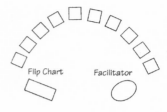

Theater style (chairs in rows facing front, no tables)

- Advantages: This is the best configuration to fit the most people in the least amount of space. It focuses on the facilitator, presenters and visual aids at the front of the room.
- Drawbacks: There is little intimacy and cohesion among participants. It is difficult to encourage interaction among participants and is not conducive to "instant" small-group breakouts if chairs are fixed. Theater style makes for an intense focus on the presenter.

When to use theater style: It is appropriate for large-group gatherings, especially when information is being delivered one way, like speeches and video presentations, and little interaction is desired. Tip: Angle the chairs, if possible, so group members can see at least a few people.

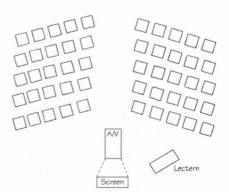

Classroom style (chairs with tables facing front — straight or at angles, or desks if the meeting literally takes place in a classroom)

- Advantages: This arrangement accommodates more people per square foot than circles or ovals, although less than theater style, and gives participants a surface for writing.
- Drawbacks: It can remind participants of being in school, which isn't always pleasant for some. It minimizes participation, since there is little eye contact or intimacy among participants, unless you angle the chairs and tables.

When to use classroom style: This works for training situations or other one-way presentations, where it is desirable for participants to take notes, and where little audience interaction is called for. Create an angle if possible.

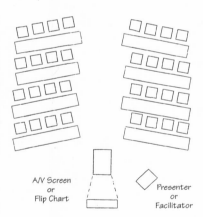

A/V Screen or Flip Chart

Presenter or Facilitator

Meetings That Occur Outside the Meeting Room

Have you ever attended a meeting where a lot was accomplished, yet very little seemed to be done in the meeting room itself? I call this the "meeting in the hall" syndrome. This often occurs when there are too many people invited, or when there are diverse opinions that are difficult to resolve in a large group. The real meeting simply happens during breaks or some other time. This is akin to the legal maneuvers of discussing things at sidebar, in the judge's chambers, or settling matters out of court.

When I worked for the Dr Pepper Company, I attended a meeting at MCA Universal that included executives from the studio and representatives for the musical group the Bee Gees. We were scheduled to negotiate a three-way tie-in promotion involving the soft drink, a Universal movie that was soon to be released *(Sgt. Pepper's Lonely Hearts Club Band)*, and a poster of the artists who appeared in the movie. Each of the three groups brought two to six advisors to the meeting.

The meeting was held in a large conference room and was characterized by much blustering and posturing, and going nowhere fast, until we took a break. During the time out, the head studio representative, the artists' manager, and I started talking about what each of us wanted, and what each of us was prepared to contribute to the tie-in promotion. In about five minutes we had an agreement. When the meeting resumed, we announced our agreement to the somewhat surprised group, and turned the focus of the meeting from fruitless wrangling to a serious discussion of how we were going to do it. If we had met separately in the first place, the larger meeting could have had focused on how to implement the details, and would have saved a lot of time as well.

By the way, the movie was a box-office flop. But we got a record number of Dr Pepper displays in grocery stores as a result of the promotion!

4

Preparation

The truth you never hear:

"Since we didn't bother to give you any material to review in advance, we're handing out the twenty-five-page study now, so we can waste everyone's time together. After a few minutes, I'll ask for your comments, which won't count for much, since there's no way you can absorb it all in a short time."

And the statement you hear all too often:

"Oops! The bulb must have blown. Well, let's see here ... does anybody know where the light switch is? Who knows how to change the bulb on these projectors? Ow! That's hot!"

The Symptoms:

Participants Are Not Prepared

You are invited to a meeting but feel uncomfortable because you are not prepared to comment intelligently on the subjects being discussed. Even if you know what the meeting is about, you and others may be at a great disadvantage if no materials are given to you in advance to review. Often, the meeting disintegrates into a rambling discussion, and the participants learn that they'll have to review or study for another meeting, when they'll finally address the real topic. The "wheels fall off" many meetings if people are not prepared beforehand.

Every Monday morning, the administrative and medical department heads attended a weekly operating meeting at County Memorial Hospital. Ed, the CEO, led these meetings, conducting them in a heavy-handed, authoritarian style. The agenda, if there was one, was seldom announced in advance, so none of the participants knew how to prepare. As a result, they came ready to discuss what they imagined were the most important issues affecting their departments. Invariably, Ed asked them to comment or report on subjects they weren't prepared to intelligently discuss.

The meetings covered whatever topics Ed felt like discussing, and often veered off in many directions. The department heads were frequently embarrassed in front of their peers, and their only consolation was that no one was spared; eventually everyone had their "turn in the barrel."

Agenda Items Not Prioritized

When agenda items are not prioritized, points of less importance often consume most or all of the time in the meeting, and the most important issues are not given the attention they deserve. Frequently, they have to be postponed until another meeting.

> The monthly board meetings of a community theater group were an exercise in futility. The president prepared an agenda based on whatever details she thought needed the board's attention. Two regular agenda items were old business and new business. Generally, these catch-all categories were an open invitation to discuss virtually anything. One evening the board spent over two hours discussing *ad nauseam* whether or not to raise the price of refreshments. Of course, there were many excursions (such as the pros and cons of ginger ale versus Seven-Up™) that seemed to make sense but were not really all that important. At that same meeting, they spent only ten minutes discussing how to increase their contributor base, which was a far more important topic.

Lack of, or Fuzzy, Ground Rules

Another frequently overlooked area is to determine the ground rules for how the meeting will be conducted. Ground rules are process-related agreements that generally apply throughout the meeting. Most ground rules cover group behavior, such as allowing only one person to talk at a time. Without deciding in advance how things will run, much is left to chance, and the meeting can slip downhill fast. In the absence of ground rules, arbitrary rules might be invented by the leader or facilitator on the spot, which can result in chaos and resentment by participants.

It is easy for meetings to bog down when there are no established ground rules for how items will be introduced to the group, how subjects will be discussed, how ideas will be collected and evaluated, how decisions will be made, and how disruptive behavior will be handled. Among the more confusing meeting imperatives are vague references to Robert's Rules of Order or parliamentary procedure, especially when the person quoting them does not have a clue to their actual meaning.

Logistics Not Covered

A final area for preparing for a meeting involves logistics. If you have attended meetings where the audio/visual equipment doesn't work (or malfunctions halfway through), the handouts aren't ready, the coffee doesn't show up, or there is no extension cord, you've witnessed how the smallest details can derail a meeting. At best, such logistics details are a nuisance. At their worst, they can effectively shut down a meeting.

At a pivotal meeting with a client, I was poised to recommend a training program for their field service personnel. Or so I thought. I had prepared visual aids to support the proposal using a popular computer presentation program. Since I did not have a laptop computer at the time, I was dependent on the computer and projection system in my client's conference room. I checked with their technician several days in advance. "No problem," the technician assured me, "we have the same software program on our system. All you have to do is bring your file on a floppy disk." I even called the software manufacturer to confirm the technician's information.

On the meeting day, I arrived an hour early just to be safe, floppy disk in hand. It was then that I learned that the presentation program was on the client's network and had to be downloaded. The technician said, "No problem ... we ought to have it downloaded in a few minutes." Forty-five minutes later, he was still struggling to download the program, as my clients arrived for the meeting. We were nowhere close to being ready, and the conference room projection system was flashing all kinds of weird computer messages. The only thing more interesting was the color draining from my face. Our only choice was to reschedule the meeting, which we did. While the client was understanding, the meeting was an unmitigated disaster. For someone who should have known better, this was a most humbling experience. Ever since then, I always double- and triple-check things whenever I hear, "No problem."

The outcome of many meetings is directly proportional to the amount of forethought and preparation that precedes them. Of course, the steps we have already covered — clarifying the purpose, determining the right people, and selecting and arranging the meeting space — are all essential steps. This chapter will cover several others.

First Aid for Planning Ahead

- Everyone attending plays a significant part in preparing for a meeting to make it more effective.
- Draw up a prioritized agenda.

- Determine the ground rules.
- Make a checklist for logistics arrangements.

Each Person Attending Should Prepare:

What Should the Leader Do Before the Meeting?

- Determine the meeting's goals and decide if the meeting is truly necessary.
- Determine who will attend, including part-time attendees. Coordinate schedules if necessary.
- Decide how much participation is desired, and how decisions will be made in the meeting.
- Appoint a facilitator and recorder. Work with the facilitator to determine the agenda and ground rules.
- Set the place, time, and dress code.
- Invite resource people and let them know specifically what you want them to do in the meeting.
- Prepare materials for participants to review prior to the meeting if it's appropriate.
- Invite participants, and provide them with as much information as possible, including the purpose, agenda, pertinent details, and advance review materials.

What Should the Facilitator Do Before the Meeting?

- Develop the agenda and ground rules with the leader.

- Plan and prepare for logistics, such as the room layout, refreshments, breakout areas, audio/visual equipment, and in-room beverages and food. If a meeting planner is assigned, work with him/her to coordinate these details.
- Develop the optimum processes for accomplishing the meeting purpose.

What Should Participants Do Before the Meeting?

- Reply to the meeting notice if requested, and note the meeting on your calendar. If the meeting is in a remote location, make travel arrangements. Plan to arrive early.
- Read any relevant materials to prepare for the meeting. Prepare a point of view of key issues.
- Give input for the agenda to the leader or facilitator, if requested.

What Should Resource People Do Before the Meeting?

- Understand fully the goals of the meeting and how your expertise can help accomplish the purpose.
- Do research and reading necessary to prepare for the meeting. Prepare materials for participants to review in advance.
- Prepare a presentation for the group, if it's appropriate. Notify the facilitator or meeting planner if audio/visual equipment is required.

Before idea-generating sessions for new products, I often ask participants to go "shopping" to observe what is happening in their related fields. They are encouraged to make notes, take pictures, or even buy things that interest them. With this kind of involvement, participants are eager to share their observations with the group and use their experiences as springboards for ideas. The night before one session, for example, our group of eight descended upon a supermarket in a strip mall. With the store manager's permission, each person carried a disposable camera. While our task was to generate ideas for new household cleaning products, everyone was encouraged to visit all parts of the store. We also went to a hardware store and a fast-food restaurant, to see if anything caught our attention. The photos were developed overnight, and we used them as springboards for different areas of exploration the next day.

Develop the Meeting Agenda

The meeting agenda is like a road map, a guide for how the goals of the meeting will be met. The leader or facilitator or both usually prepare an agenda. They must identify all the issues, decide which ones are most important, and finally nail down how much time each issue is worth.

If you are dependent on others for agenda items — as is often the case in team, committee, or staff meetings — ask participants in advance for the issues they wish to discuss, assigning a priority to each and deciding how much time they require. This advance poll can be done by phone, fax, e-mail, or memo and saves time at the meeting. It also requires participants to consider how they wish to use the group's time on their behalf and encourages people to come prepared.

After the items have been collected, build an agenda with time blocks assigned, starting with the most important items first. These are usually, but not always, the items for which the largest amount of time has been requested.

Here is a sample agenda for a staff meeting:

Group:	Research Department Staff Meeting
Meeting Date:	December 10
Purpose of Meeting:	Generate ideas for new office layout; update on key projects
Facilitator:	Marcia

Time	Topics/Process	Discussion Leader
9:00 - 9:30	Idea generation: How to utilize the new space most effectively. Free-flow for ten minutes, then directed idea generation for twenty minutes.	G.B.
9:30 - 9:40	Sort out and prioritize ideas.	Marcia
9:40 - 9:50	Reach consensus, determine action steps on best ideas.	Group
9:50 - 10:00	Update on budget process	Gary
10:00 - 10:10	New project assignments	Linda
10:10 - 10:20	Travel schedule update	Group
10:20 - 10:30	General interest items; end	G.B.

Several word processing programs make agenda making quite easy. For example, Microsoft Word 6.0 has an Agenda Wizard™. This document template generates an agenda based on answers to questions it asks the user. See the Appendix for more sample agendas for other types of meetings.

Establish Ground Rules

Ground rules are decisions that members agree to live by during meetings to make the process run smoothly. Many groups have unclear or unspoken ground rules for meetings which are, through trial and error, learned by all participants over time. By examining how you "do" meetings, however, and making the ground rules clear, your meetings can run smoothly and efficiently.

While the leader or facilitator (or both) might be chosen to draw up a list of ground rules, every member of the group must agree to abide by them. This is one area where consensus is mandatory.

For groups that meet regularly, the ground rules should be reviewed occasionally — every few months or so — or when the need arises. For ad hoc or newly forming groups, one of the first priorities should be to establish the ground rules by which the group will operate.

Here are some ground rules from different groups that you may want to consider adopting for your meetings:

- Meetings will start and end on time, unless the group agrees to extend.
- There is only one meeting; no side conversations — only one person may talk at a time.
- All viewpoints are valid; no one will be criticized for expressing an opinion.
- Ideas will be generated and collected first, evaluated later.
- The facilitator is in charge of the meeting process; the role of facilitator will be rotated each meeting.

- Decisions will be made by consensus whenever possible; voting is a last resort. (See Chapter 9.) Decisions made by the group will be supported by all members.
- All group members will learn and practice constructive meeting skills. (See Chapter 6.)
- Presenters and resource people will prepare advance review materials whenever possible. Group members will review materials sent to them (or complete assignments) in advance of meetings.

To get started, review the ground rules for your meetings already in effect, even the ones that haven't been officially adopted. Examine these rules to confirm that they are actually useful and that everyone is comfortable with them. If you want to make changes, try out a few new ground rules and see if they make the process more effective. After you have experimented with new rules, introduce others when the group is ready. Finally, give a copy of the ground rules to everyone involved and post them in the meeting room.

Make a Checklist for Logistics Planning

The final step to cover in planning for meetings is logistics. This is one area where it is easy to assume that someone else is handling the details. It is easy to be lulled into complacency, especially if you have experienced a streak of good luck when several meetings have already run smoothly. My experience has been that well-coordinated logistics happen not because of good luck but through careful preparation.

Besides selecting the appropriate room and arranging the furniture to fit the meeting's purpose, there are dozens of other logistics details which need the attention of leaders and facilitators. Your checklist might include:

Arrange for, inspect, and try out audio/visual equipment.

- Be very specific about the equipment you order, such as the brand name and model of the slide or overhead projector you like best. For overheads, I always specify a two-bulb projector, which gives me a built-in backup should a bulb blow.
- If you are using computer-projected visuals, bring your own equipment (laptop and projector or panel) and hookups.
- Request backup equipment. Depending on the type of audio/visual support you need, arrange for a backup projector, spare bulbs, and even an alternate way to display visuals. For example, I made a set of overhead transparencies as a backup for a presentation where I was using my laptop computer. Ten minutes before the presentation, the computer system went crazy and simply stopped. Rather than panicking, I decided to use the overhead transparencies and acted as if nothing had ever happened. The presentation went fine. Now I always make a backup.
- Check out all equipment on site as soon as you arrive, and again just before the meeting starts.

Build a meeting "kit." Your kit might include:

- Extension cords.
- Markers for flip charts — the "non-lethal" kind that smell good and don't bleed through.
- Pads and pencils or pens for all participants, unless you ask them to bring their own.
- Name tags — even for an ongoing group if there are new people attending.
- Blank transparencies (if you're using overheads) with markers that work on film.
- Masking tape and pins for affixing flip charts to walls (my meeting kit includes rope and clothes-pins in case tape or tacks cannot be used on the walls).
- Wide duct tape for taping down wires that someone might trip over.
- A selection of connectors for the computer.
- Materials for exercises, if appropriate.
- A stopwatch, or a watch with a second hand, for the timekeeper.

Make sure that all written materials, such as handouts, workbooks and leave-behinds, are prepared and delivered to the meeting room beforehand.

- Materials that are going to be distributed to the participants should be prepared well in advance and brought personally to the meeting site by the presenter, facilitator, leader or planner.

- The only failsafe method for assuring delivery of materials is to personally carry them to the meeting. Materials checked as baggage on airlines have ended up in different cities. Despite "positively, absolutely" overnight express service, hotel clerks have denied ever receiving materials for which they have personally signed, and so on. And don't even think you can depend on the hotel photocopier!

- If you have handouts for a meeting in an off-site location that are too bulky for you to hand-carry, send half of them by one service (such as Federal Express) and the other half by another (like Airborne). If one service fails to deliver on time, at least you will have handouts for every other person, which can be shared.

Arrange for breaks and refreshments. Successful meetings include specific times for participants to relax, release and recharge. Maslow was right: the basic human needs that go unsatisfied take precedence over everything else. It is difficult to think creatively or focus on critical issues if you have to go to the bathroom, or when you are hungry or sleepy. This may seem like a profound statement of the obvious, yet I am amazed at the number of meetings that rattle on and on with no end in sight, and no relief for the weary.

- If breaks are not planned, what often happens is that people take breaks on their own, or tune out mentally, which is just as bad. The antidote is to plan frequent breaks as part of the agenda, about every hour — or no less than every ninety minutes.

- A break does not have to mean a twenty-minute scattering of the group, which then turns into a half-hour. Instead, a three- to five-minute stand-up break in the meeting room is often just what everyone needs.
- Refreshments are usually included with breaks and may also be available to participants during the meeting. Many people use food as an incentive to get others to attend meetings.
- Water should be available at all times in the meeting room, with other beverages as desired, such as coffee, tea, juices and soft drinks.
- Light snacks may be made available throughout, or only during breaks. Be careful of plying meeting participants with too much sugar or high-fat snacks. They tend to produce a fleeting high, followed by lethargy. Fresh fruit, water, juices, pretzels, and low-fat cookies or crackers are nice alternatives.

Handle visual and sound distractions. Well before meeting participants arrive, designate someone to "walk the room," observing anything that might distract people from fully participating in the meeting. Look and listen for things such as:

- Lines of vision that are blocked (change the room arrangement if possible).
- A loud heater blower or ventilation system that makes it difficult to hear one another (turn it off during the meeting, or change rooms if possible).
- Beautiful yet distracting views outside the window (pull the curtains for part of the meeting; open them at the break).

By "pre-experiencing" your meeting, you will become aware of things which support the meeting purpose and things which do not.

Recap of Part I

Before moving on, remember that an ounce of planning is worth a ton of excuses. At the very minimum, remember the four P's:

- *Purpose* — Know why you are meeting.
- *People* — Make sure the right participants attend.
- *Place* — Choose a room and set it up to serve your purpose.
- *Preparation* — Create a prioritized agenda, make sure people come prepared, and plan for logistics.

Part II

During the Meeting:
The Four F's of Flow

" Let's review it, one more time."

During the Meeting:
The Four F's of Flow

5. Focus

Prioritize the agenda items, work the agenda to stay on track, be aware of time, record ideas and decisions.

6. Facilitation

Encourage all the participants to use effective facili-tating skills to keep the group involved. Appoint a facilitator to run the meeting process.

7. Feedback

Observe and respond to ongoing feedback during the meeting. Separate generating ideas from evaluating ideas. Learn how to sort and prioritize ideas, then use a balanced response technique to give feedback and turn ideas into solutions.

8. Fun and Fellowship

Use humor and laughter to lighten things up while getting serious work done. Get to know each other as people.

5

Focus

The truth you never hear:

"Following our usual pattern, our meeting today will probably get off-track after the first few minutes, and we'll ramble on for several hours until it's totally out of control."

The Symptoms:

Group Members Not on Board

In most meetings, it is safe to assume that not all members share the same level of interest, understanding, and enthusiasm for the purpose or the agenda items. For any number of reasons, people come to a meeting with other priorities or even personal issues which can influence or overwhelm their participation.

For any single issue or discussion item, some group members will know more than others, and everyone will view it through his or her own experience and "filters." If some means is not introduced to establish a common starting point, there is a good chance that the discussion will ramble and drift before everyone is on board. Body language — especially puzzled or bored expressions — are a dead giveaway.

Agenda Items Not Managed

Even with a planned agenda, meetings can quickly lose their focus if the group drifts off into other directions. We've already noted that a prioritized agenda includes identifying all the relevant issues for the group, deciding which ones are most important, and figuring out the time required for each. Simply writing an agenda is not enough, however. A piece of paper will not, by itself, keep the discussion on track or control disruptive behavior.

When meetings lose their focus, I've discovered that most people don't speak up to alert other group members about what is happening. More often, if time runs out before all agenda items are covered, the meeting just keeps on going, and going, and going....

The discussion can be moving along smoothly, when all of a sudden something happens to throw the meeting out of focus. Perhaps someone interrupts with a tangent or wanders off on a lengthy "war story," and the discussion leapfrogs into a completely different direction. Sometimes, the group never gets back to the real agenda.

The weekly operating committee meetings of Smithson Food Company were exasperating to most who attended. They were always held on Monday, and it seemed to take hours for the group to focus on what was important. Instead, the group talked about anything that happened to pop up. Some issues were handled in a minute or two, while others took much longer. One staff member suggested the group prepare agendas for the meetings. What they soon discovered was that making an agenda was only part of the solution.

In a typical meeting, Doug, the always-efficient assistant to the president, would barge in and say something like, "Are you aware that a truckload of product had to be diverted in Chicago due to the Teamsters' strike? We may miss the promotion date." Lurch! For the next two hours or so, the operating committee would then focus on solving this crisis, forgetting whatever else might be on the meeting agenda.

Of course, the issues that Doug brought up were important, and it was true that most of the committee members would not be aware of the crisis situation. It turned out that Doug received calls from different field salespeople every Monday morning, minutes before the weekly meeting. As a result, the topics were not included in the agenda, which was prepared the previous Friday. Doug felt it was his responsibility to bring the "crisis of the week" to the committee's attention.

Similar scenarios were played out almost every Monday, and none of the committee members ever questioned whether dealing with the "crisis of the day" was the best use of their time, whether other items might have a higher priority, or even if it was appropriate for the operating committee to deal with the issue. It is no wonder they were all frustrated with the meetings — everybody except Doug, that is!

Group's Output Not Recorded

It is easy for meetings to lose focus when important ideas, issues and action steps are not captured when they come up. Group members can easily forget about what has been discussed, and the meeting may become repetitive or get bogged down. If they are not recorded, good ideas and potential solutions can "fall off the table," never to reappear. Even when there is a recorder to take notes, group members may not know what is being captured or lost until the minutes are printed, sometimes days later. By then, it may be too late to recapture important discussions or decisions. Most people will have forgotten by then.

Group Energy is Low

You've been there. After a couple of hours of batting around ideas or analyzing an issue, you feel drained. The few people still involved in the discussion do not seem to notice that you and several others have tuned out. You begin to wonder if you are the only one who is fatigued. Doesn't anyone else have to go to the bathroom? When energy is low, group members easily lose their focus, and little is accomplished.

First Aid for Staying Focused:

- Establish a common starting point at the beginning of the meeting.
- Pay attention to the agenda during the meeting: follow priorities, intervene when necessary, use a timekeeper, and dump wandering discussions in a "parking lot."

- Track the meeting using "group notes."
- Use breaks, energizers and other techniques to allow the group to recharge and refocus.
- Stay focused as a participant.

Establish a Common Starting Point

It is the leader's or facilitator's job to remind all participants why the meeting is being held (purpose), why each participant has been invited (people), and to preview the agenda and time contract (preparation). This will set the stage for the meeting and help ensure that everyone is starting at the same place. If advance materials have been distributed, it may be appropriate to briefly recap highlights. If group members have different levels of expertise and understanding, one of the initial agenda items might be a summary of key information to "level the playing field."

Work the Agenda — Make Priorities

An agenda with strict priorities is the major tool to maintain focus in a meeting. Earlier, we used the analogy of the agenda as a road map — to be useful, the facilitator or other members must check it frequently to ensure that the meeting stays on course and "in focus."

- As a reminder, when designing the agenda, assign each item a designated priority and estimate the time it will take to discuss, forge ideas, evaluate or make decisions. Start by assuming each item will take five minutes or less, unless more time is specifically requested.

- If an agenda has not been developed in advance, make it the first order of business. If group members are responsible for discussion items, go around and ask everyone for his/her top priority and time requested. A second go-round gets the second priority, and a third time gathers the third-ranking concerns.

- Post the agenda items on a flip chart sheet, or make a copy for each participant. At the beginning of the meeting, ask if there are any additional items. If so, assign a priority and time estimate, and add them to the list.

- Start with the first item and complete each one before moving to the next, with the timekeeper noting the time spent discussing each item.

- When the timekeeper reminds the group that time is up for an item, the facilitator asks the group (or the leader) to decide if they want to continue on, or bring that issue to a close. If more time is needed, be specific; for example, "We need fifteen more minutes on this."

- After all top items are covered, move to the second-priority items, then on to the third. Remember, if any items run overtime, you will most likely not have enough time to cover everything. This is why you make priorities: the most important items get covered first.

- Recognizing that time estimates are only a guess, save ten or fifteen minutes at the end of the meeting to cover any last-minute "must-cover" and "parking lot" items.

Work the Agenda — Intervene to Keep on Track

It is normal for most meetings to veer off course at some point; after all, we are human, and most meetings are a dynamic and unrehearsed process. Before the meeting is allowed to disintegrate, however, someone must intervene and call for a mid-course correction. While that someone is usually the facilitator, any group member can intervene.

- If the meeting strays from the topic being discussed, the facilitator or any other group member may bring this fact to the group's attention. The group can then decide to keep discussing the side issue or return to the agenda. The key is awareness; knowing how the group is spending its time and why. For example, "Folks, we are talking about a side issue here, which is taking time away from other agenda items. Let's make sure we are using our time to stay on the agenda and cover the most important items."

- One way to stay focused when asking for opinions or reactions from everyone is to allow a set time — say, one or two minutes — for comments from each participant. The time-keeper can simply raise his or her hand to notify each speaker when their time is up. This will encourage each member to be concise and stay on the subject. Remember to build this response time into the agenda when preparing it.

- If someone brings up a new subject or a non-agenda item, try the "parking lot" technique. Start a flip chart page with the title "Parking Lot." Any time an item is brought up that is off the subject, suggest that it go into the parking lot, and post it on the sheet. At the end of the meeting, allow time to address items in the parking lot, even if the action is to defer them until a later meeting.

Use the Timekeeper to Keep Focused

As noted earlier, the timekeeper plays a key role in keeping a meeting on track. The timekeeper's job should be rotated among group members. Here are some other ways the timekeeper can help a meeting stay focused.

- Using a stopwatch or wristwatch with a second hand, the timekeeper notes when specific agenda items begin and end. If discussions run close to the allotted time, that is all that is required — there is no sense quibbling over a minute or two. However, when time is almost up on an issue, the timekeeper lets the group know. It is up to the group, with the help of the facilitator, to decide to keep on the issue or move on. For example, the group may want to get through the rest of the agenda and then revisit the extended issue at the end of the meeting. In some groups, the leader may make this decision. If it is important enough, a separate meeting may be called to discuss an issue in more detail, which would also give people time to prepare better for meaningful discussion.

- The timekeeper should refrain from making judgments — he/she is not the facilitator; his/her job is simply to serve the group by monitoring the time.
- The timekeeper may also alert the facilitator and group members of break times and overall meeting time. For example, "As a reminder, we have ten minutes left before we break." Time reminders may also be written on cards and held up by the timekeeper to remind the presenter or facilitator.

Track the Meeting Using "Group Notes"

Many people incorrectly assume that the role of the recorder is similar to a court reporter — taking down word for word everything that is said in a meeting. This could be the main reason some people never volunteer for the job! Capturing everything verbatim would be very difficult without stenography skills or a tape recorder to use for transcribing. Unfortunately, most group members do not know if the information logged is accurate until long after the meeting is over, when they receive a copy of the minutes.

It is far more productive and useful to group members when the recorder documents and displays key ideas, decisions, consensus agreements and action steps as they are discussed. The "group notes" method is the way to make this happen.

- The most important skills for a recorder are the ability to listen and summarize accurately without evaluating.
- Group notes are headlines and summary points (or even drawings) written on a flip chart or white board. Everyone is able to see the meeting output as it happens, and to confirm the accuracy of information.
- The recorder numbers each sheet of the group notes and hangs the sheets on the wall for quick reference as the meeting progresses. Tip: Change colors of markers for different topics; this makes the group notes more fun and vivid.
- The facilitator can use group notes to remind the participants of what has already been covered, which minimizes repetition. For example, if someone revisits an issue already covered, the facilitator can simply refer to the group notes and say something like, "Ed, we've already covered this in some detail. Do you have any new insights to add?"
- Recorders also must be able to write fast and legibly. Being able to draw simple graphics is a plus. If a computer is used for taking group notes, the recorder must be able to type fast.
- Being able to spell can be useful, but more

important is to not be afraid of making spelling mistakes as you go — they can always be corrected later.

- The recorder should not be reluctant to ask group members for help, if he/she gets behind in recording items. Ultimately, group members are responsible for ensuring that the group notes accurately reflect ideas, decisions and action steps.

- Technology permits rapid note-taking with computers, and projection devices are available which can display the information. However, since only one "screen" is seen at a time, the screens must be scrolled in order to recall what has already been recorded, which is not as effective as group notes, which are on constant display.

- "White boards," or electronic easels, may also be used for the group notes. Some products transfer the writing straight to a computer or copier device, which generates letter-size pages that can be duplicated and distributed. Other devices shrink regular flip chart pages into letter-size pages, which can be copied and distributed to members.

Plan Frequent Breaks and Energizers

Most people need some kind of break at regular intervals to maintain their focus during a meeting. Let's face it: some of us have shorter attention spans — and smaller

bladders — than others! Breaks and energizers help participants recharge, and provide an opportunity to refocus the
meeting. Here are some suggestions for breaks and energizers to keep your meeting focused and flowing:

- Try to change something about every twenty
  minutes. This can be as simple as changing the
  subject, or the methods of participating. For
  example, the facilitator might go around the
  room and ask for others' viewpoints on a subject
  that has been monopolized by a few people.
- Ask presenters to break their material into
  fifteen- or twenty-minute "chunks," with time
  for questions or discussion after each segment.
  This provides another opportunity to summarize
  what has been covered and concentrate on what
  is coming up.
- Have a ground rule that allows any member to
  call a mini-break anytime he or she senses that
  the group is dragging or is low in energy. After
  the mini-break, remember to zero in on the
  subject, perhaps by summarizing what has
  happened so far, emphasizing points of
  agreement and restating the purpose of the
  meeting.
- The facilitator can keep group members
  involved, and therefore focused, in several ways.
  For example, ask members at random to
  summarize discussions, to interpret information

addressing their own area of responsibility, or for opinions that support or differ from a common point of view.

- Plan a formal break every hour or hour and a half. Plan for no more than ten to fifteen minutes, which allows enough time for most people to stretch, grab a refreshment, and go to the bathroom. The longer a meeting goes without a break, the longer the break should be. However, if the break is too long, it is tempting for many group members to get involved in other things, such as checking messages or returning phone calls. When the meeting begins again after the break, refocus by reviewing agenda items covered and previewing those remaining.

- Energizers and games are widely used by trainers and many facilitators and can enhance any meeting. For example, a brain-teaser or puzzle is a good energizer to get people thinking in non-traditional ways prior to an idea-generating session. See more ideas in Chapter 8.

- Get in the habit of starting meetings on time. Enforcing this discipline will encourage members to be more concise and to ramble less. You may have to start with several people not present when you decide to initiate this ground rule. After a few times, most people will make the effort to show up on time.

One board where I served held its meetings in members' homes. Because of this, the members spent the first fifteen minutes or so of each meeting social-izing. Rather than discontinue the social time, we simply established that the social period began at 7:00 p.m. and then started the meeting at 7:15. It worked.

- Post the purpose of the meeting on a sheet of flip chart paper or on printed agendas for each participant. This reminds participants of why they are meeting.

- Establish the ground rule of "only one meeting — no side conversations." This helps to keep everyone on the same agenda. These types of ground rules act as a neutral authority that the facilitator can refer to.

- Take a progress check midway through the meeting. Recap agenda items covered, and those remaining. Make any mid-course corrections to keep the meeting focused on the purpose. The facilitator should do this anytime he/she senses that the group needs to get refocused on the purpose of the meeting.

- If people arrive after the meeting has begun, a practice which should not be encouraged, refer them to the group notes to bring them up to speed on what has transpired. If you stop the meeting to update latecomers, it might reinforce their behavior. The simple act of starting every meeting on time will go a long way to discourage latecomers.

- In training meetings, stop after a block of information has been covered, usually about twenty minutes or so. Go around the room and ask participants to recap one or two things they learned which will be most helpful to them. This "group summary" will reinforce the learning, and let the trainer know what is being retained. It also provides a launching point to concentrate on the next training segment.

Staying Focused as a Participant

We have emphasized the roles of the leader, timekeeper, recorder, and especially the facilitator in keeping a meeting focused on its purpose and agenda. What about participants? If participants stay involved in the meeting, the work of every other role is much easier. In many respects, the responsibilities of participants are the most important. Here are some ways for participants to stay focused:

- Prepare by reading materials sent in advance to review; prepare a point of view, questions, and opinions.
- After understanding the purpose of the meeting, determine your own goals. What do you want to accomplish in the meeting? How will the information or ideas impact your area of responsibility?

- Take the meeting seriously. Show up on time, and be involved throughout the meeting. If you have other pressing priorities (and who doesn't?), set them aside during the meeting.
- Practice active listening during the meeting by concentrating on speakers with your eyes, and fully responding to what is going on.
- When you voice an opinion or concern, know where you are going before you start. Make sure your comments are relevant to the subject being discussed.
- Learn and practice skills that help maintain group harmony or keep the group on task. See the next chapter for more details.

6

Facilitation

"Let's just ramble out of control for the next two hours. Say whatever pops into your mind, whether it's on the agenda or not. It won't make any difference anyway, because everyone knows these meetings are a joke. Since no one is in charge, feel free to take control whenever you feel like it."

The Symptoms:

The Meeting is Out of Control

Things seem to hum along in the meeting, up to a point. There is a purpose, and the group starts out by following an agenda. Without a facilitator, however, there is no one to guide the discussion, keep the group focused, and take charge when the discussion drifts. As a result, the more expressive people get the most "air time" and slant the discussion toward their point of view. People start telling war stories. Side issues surface. More often than we like to admit, the meeting turns into an energy-draining free-for-all, with little accomplished.

By the second hour of a day-long school board retreat, the group sensed that they were in for a very long session. The president decided to shake things up and not run the meeting as he usually did. Instead, he said he wanted to be a "fly on the wall" and simply listen. But since he did not appoint a facilitator, no one was in charge.

This event was a planning retreat for the school board, and the group's task was to come up with ideas that would make the board more responsive to the community and the needs of students. However, because there was no facilitator for the retreat, no ground rules were established, and the meeting stumbled along.

The problem was not preparation. In fact, every board member came equipped with several ideas. Yet at several points, it seemed that each person was more interested in making sure his or her ideas were heard and carried out, rather than working toward a common goal. This meant that the discussion often veered off in different directions. Ultimately the result was that the board members were mentally and physically drained midway through the morning of the first day.

This meeting was going nowhere fast, like a ship without a captain, or even a rudder. Shortly after lunch, the president called an early end to the retreat, because it was clear that very little was going to be accomplished.

Some Group Members are Excluded

Some people have attended meetings which become debilitating experiences for them because they seem to be excluded from the proceedings. The leader or facilitator seldom calls on them, so it is difficult for them to "break into" the flow of the conversation. Without a strong sense of participation, they might eventually withdraw and generally cannot wait until the meeting is over. Worse, sometimes when they finally offer ideas or suggestions, they are often crushed by negative responses, which makes them withdraw even further.

Over-controlled Meetings

Good facilitators know how and when to intervene and guide a group through its agenda without being heavy-handed. It requires a delicate balance to avoid crossing the line into over-managing the process. Symptoms of over-controlled meetings include strict adherence to rules such as parliamentary procedure, leaders or facilitators who do more talking than listening, and other autocratic behavior. Another problem occurs when leaders take meeting management to the extreme by micro-managing every last detail. Most people do not respond well to over-controlled meetings. They feel manipulated or useless and "tune out" quickly.

While a heavy-handed approach might seem like an efficient way to run a meeting, it is clearly not the best way to get the group members involved and committed.

First Aid for Facilitating:

- Train all group members in group process and facilitation skills.
- Learn positive "meeting language" and encourage all group members to use it.
- Designate a facilitator for every meeting.
- Separate the role of meeting leader from the role of facilitator.

Train Group Members in Group Process and Facilitator Skills

While I have observed several facilitators who lead groups intuitively, most of them do not possess some mystical powers — they have simply taken the time to learn and practice basic skills. Any organization that holds meetings will benefit by having a cadre of trained people who are available to facilitate meetings. For ongoing teams and any group that meets regularly, I recommend that every team member learn basic facilitator skills.

A significant benefit of having several people trained in group process and facilitator skills is that your meetings will take a quantum leap in effectiveness. The reason? Facilitators also make excellent group participants, because of their keen awareness of the tools that make meetings productive. Some of my most enjoyable and fruitful meetings happened with other trained facilitators.

What are the skills that an effective meeting facilitator should learn and refine? My top ten list includes:

1. The ability to remain neutral and objective throughout the meeting. This means not showing favoritism toward any individual or idea.

2. Having high energy and being able to keep the group involved and energized throughout the meeting.

3. Being assertive without being abrasive. This requires sensing when to intervene and when to back off and let things take their course.

4. The ability to listen well, and to know when the meeting is veering off the subject or otherwise not moving toward accomplishing its purpose.

5. An unwavering dedication to serving the needs of the group. This includes checking in with the leader and other group members often to confirm that they are satisfied with what is happening and how their time is being spent. This always means putting the group's interests ahead of any personal interests.

6. The ability to encourage participation among all group members while making each person comfortable. This requires recognizing and honoring the fact that people have different styles of thinking and communicating.

7. The capability to create a safe, open, trusting and supportive environment for all group members.

8. Being able to recognize and deal with hidden agendas and disruptive behaviors.

9. Being alert to group "membership" issues, especially for people who are new to the group.
10. Having a sense of humor and knowing when and
    how to use it effectively in the meeting.

Beyond these general skills are specific group process
functions which are designed to nurture good relationships
among members and keep the meeting focused. While
mastering these functions is a must for facilitators, these
functions should also be learned and practiced by all group
members.

Group Maintenance Functions

These are process skills that build or keep good relationships among members of the group.

- Building and crediting: This skill involves
  adding onto or modifying others' ideas or
  suggestions and making them stronger while
  giving them credit. This is one of the most
  powerful techniques you can use in meetings.
- Encouraging: Being friendly, positive and
  responsive to members and their contributions,
  without showing favoritism.
- Expressing group feelings: Sensing moods,
  feelings and relationships in the group; relieving
  tension with appropriate use of humor.
- Harmonizing: Getting people to explore their
  differences and appreciate each other's point of
  view; for example, suggesting that two people

who disagree get together at the break to find a mutually acceptable solution.

- Gate-keeping: Encouraging participation by keeping the channels of communication open.
- Observing: Sharing observed data about the process of the meeting. Also, being aware of physical dynamics such as heat, ventilation, hard chairs, and finding ways to relieve the discomfort, such as taking a break.

Task Skills

These are process skills that help keep the group focused on the meeting's purpose.

- Clarifying: Interpreting or reflecting ideas or suggestions, clearing up confusion, reminding everyone of the issue before the group.
- Summarizing: Pulling together related ideas, restating suggestions after the group has discussed them, identifying areas of agreement, and offering a recommendation or conclusion for the group to accept or reject.
- Initiating: Suggesting a procedure or ways to solve a problem, proposing tasks or goals for the group to consider.
- Information giving and seeking: Offering facts or relevant information about issues being discussed; seeking information and data from others.

- Opinion giving and seeking: Offering a belief, giving ideas, speculations and options; asking for suggestions and ideas.
- Consensus-building and testing: Moving the group toward common agreement by identifying or isolating the things everyone agrees on, then finding ways to resolve disagreements.
- Time management: Acting on input from the timekeeper to use time productively and to end the meeting within the agreed-upon time.

In conducting train-the-facilitator seminars, I have observed that it is easy to identify the skills facilitators use to run productive meetings. Nevertheless, it is more difficult to learn the skills and know how and when to use them while handling a meeting.

Getting Started with Facilitator Training

If anyone in your group has facilitator experience or training, ask if he/she would be willing to conduct the initial training for other group members. Other options include sending one or more people to training courses, or bringing in a skilled trainer to conduct in-house train-the-facilitator sessions.

Regardless of the initial training, the best way to learn and reinforce facilitator and group process skills is through practice. Fortunately, your group is likely to have frequent meetings to provide the practice opportunities. New facilitators will need and appreciate the understanding, patience and tolerance of other group members while they polish their skills.

In these practice sessions, appoint one person to be a process observer. His/her job is to observe how interactions are handled in the meeting versus what is actually being done. This would include noting when guidance and intervention by the facilitator and other members is necessary to keep the meeting on track, as well as group membership and maintenance issues. Immediately following the meeting, the process observer leads a discussion to share their observations with other members. Suggestion: Focus on what worked and what can be done to make the group more cohesive next meeting.

Develop and Encourage
Positive "Meeting Language"

Positive meeting language is purposeful and empowering to all group members. Eventually each member and facilitator should develop his/her own vocabulary, so it does not sound scripted or contrived. Here are some examples of positive meeting language to get you thinking in the right direction:

Process Skill	*Language*
Building and crediting	"Hitchhiking on Jane's suggestion of automating the packing, why don't we look at automating the whole process?"
Encouraging	"Terrific concept, Patti. Who can see a way to incorporate this in your department?"

Expressing group feelings	"We're beginning to drag a little; what do you say we take a quick break?"
Harmonizing	"Let's remember that every opinion is valid. While we all may not agree on everything at first, it is important to get everyone's input. Then we can decide how to proceed."
Gatekeeping	"Tim, you're new to this division. Your observations will be valuable to us...care to comment?"
Observing	"Hey, we did a great job in coming up with some fresh approaches. Good show!"
Clarifying	"Agnes, are you saying that the equipment is unaffordable, or it's just not in this year's budget?"
Summarizing	"Let's take a moment to see where we stand. We have all agreed on [whatever] and have yet to tackle the budget."
Initiating	"Let's go around the room and get everyone's reaction."
Information giving	"My department did a study on that about six months ago. One of the things we found...."
Information seeking	"Does anyone know if our customers think this is important?"

Opinion giving	"This solution would make life easier in my department. Let's work on making it affordable."
Opinion seeking	"Bob, do you think this would fly with the engineering department?"
Consensus building and testing	"Let's see where we stand on this. Is there anyone who can't live with the ABC strategy?" or "Is everybody comfortable with this strategy?"
Time management	"Our time is almost up. How do you want to spend the remaining fifteen minutes?"
Get meeting on track	"Let's put these side issues in the 'parking lot' for now, and focus on completing the personnel recommendation."
Control disruptive behavior (side conversations)	"Remember our ground rule for one conversation at time. The recorder won't be able to capture all the ideas if everyone talks at once."

Designate a Facilitator for Every Meeting

One of the best ways to accelerate a group's progress is by appointing a facilitator for every meeting. This will provide "on-the-job" learning for facilitators-in-training and will heighten every member's awareness of good meeting skills.

The facilitator role should be rotated among every member who has been trained or is in training. One way to "break in" people who are new to facilitation is to have them start with handling only a portion of the meeting. Be sure to assign a process observer to give feedback.

For longer meetings, a team facilitating approach works well — break the meeting into segments and have two or more facilitators take turns. This allows one person to charge their batteries while observing or participating in the meeting, while another person facilitates. Once group members have experienced the benefits of well-facilitated meetings, they will never want to hold a meeting any other way.

Separate Facilitator and Leader Roles

Many meetings run amuck when the leader, who is the boss or authority figure, also acts as the facilitator for the meeting. This bears repeating here, because of its importance. Leaders naturally have a vested interest in the outcome, which makes it difficult if not impossible to fulfill the most important facilitator trait: remaining neutral and objective throughout the meeting.

Here are some additional reasons to separate the roles:

• With a separate facilitator presiding over the meeting, the leader is free to contribute information and ideas as a full participant. He/she can also focus on listening to the ideas and contributions of others without having to worry about how the meeting is running.

- While the facilitator is in charge of the meeting process, the leader is still responsible for the outcome of the meeting. A facilitator is not a decision-maker; he/she is only responsible for running the process of the meeting.
- Participants will open up and contribute more if the leader/boss is not running the meeting. When people fully participate in the process, they have a stronger investment in the outcome. A true consensus is more likely to emerge from a group whose members are totally engaged.

If the facilitator is in charge of the meeting, what, then, is the role of the leader? Without having to worry about running the meeting, the leader is able to listen more and play a part in the meeting. While there is no need to be neutral, it is best if the leader listens to input from other group members before expressing his or her own viewpoint. Most leaders who turn over facilitating to others are able to relax more and enjoy the benefits of higher-quality and more honest input from group members.

7

Feedback

The truth you never hear:

"Well, we managed to blow off another three hours today with little to show for it, except to learn the latest chapter in Suzie's ongoing melodrama with the manufacturing department. Most of the other reports were full of the usual buzz words and jargon, with little real substance. We also managed to kill every idea that was suggested, in record time. Despite our efforts to go on as many tangents as possible, we only went an hour and ten minutes over schedule. We now have eight separate plans of action, narrowed down from the two we started with!"

The Symptoms:

Facilitator/Presenters Do Not Respond to Ongoing Feedback

If facilitators and presenters do not observe and respond to ongoing feedback from group members, they are missing a big opportunity to make the meeting more productive. This kind of feedback is not necessarily spoken out loud yet "speaks" loudly through body language and eye contact, or the lack of it. Participants who are counting ceiling tiles, examining the insides of their eyelids, or doodling on their notepads are sending clear signals. If the group isn't responding, presenters or facilitators may find themselves talking to the walls before too long.

Ideas are Crushed as They are Offered

Another symptom occurs when ideas are judged as they are brought up. Many of us are conditioned to give instant negative feedback to the ideas and suggestions of others. Maybe we react negatively because we want to show how smart we are, or we simply wish to assert ourselves. I am convinced that most of us do not intend harm when we judge others' ideas and are often unaware of what we're doing. It is simply a knee-jerk reaction that is hard to break.

The energy in the room was electric. Hal had asked some of the best and brightest people in the company to attend what he called a "green-light session," to brainstorm ideas for improving customer service. The session was held in a nice resort, and the dress was casual. In fact, it had all the elements for a successful meeting. Each of us came prepared with a supply of ideas and insights related to customer service in our area.

Hal asked each of us to share a few ideas to start things off. Jackson was first. He suggested that we pinpoint our best customers and build better relationships with them by finding out how we can serve them better. Hal smiled, then answered that we might be better off focusing on getting new customers, since we should already know what our current customers like. Jackson nodded in reluctant agreement, although he confided to me later that we didn't have a clue about the needs of our most important customers.

Maureen presented a plan for trimming our order-filling time from fourteen to five days. To carry out the new system, computer hardware upgrades and new software would be required. Hal almost leapt out of his chair. "Maureen, we just spent a ton of money last year for new computers, with little to show for it. How can we justify spending even more?" After some discussion, illustrated by excellent backup numbers, Maureen convinced Hal that we should at least test her idea in one region.

It was Rolf's turn next. He was proud of the homework he had done, leading him to suggest several ideas for improving communications with customers through a newsletter and an on-line forum. Hal's response was cordial, but he pointed out that the company tried a newsletter about five years ago, before Rolf's time, and it didn't do any good. Before Rolf could answer, Hal admonished the group, saying, "This is supposed to be a collection of the best thinkers we have in the company. So far, we're not getting very many good ideas. I hope the rest of you come up with something better."

The meeting dragged on for several painful hours. Every idea that was suggested was immediately evaluated by Hal, and most of his feedback was disapproving. After a while most group members felt very uncomfortable and simply stopped offering any more ideas. One by one everyone closed down and were finally relieved when the "brainstorming" retreat was over. If this was a green-light session, maybe Hal was color blind!

The problem with giving "instant" negative responses to ideas is threefold:

- Ideas die in their infancy, and many good ones will be lost forever.
- People tend to shut down when their ideas get crushed and may even become hostile or attempt to thwart the purpose of the meeting.
- The number of ideas is greatly reduced when each is evaluated as it is offered. It is a little like driving with the brakes on.

No Procedure to Evaluate, Sort and Prioritize the Best Ideas

How many times have you been in a meeting where dozens or even hundreds of ideas are brought up, only to learn later that no decisions were made about which ideas were best, and ultimately no action was taken? While generating ideas needs to be separated from evaluating them, eventually ideas must be sorted out and prioritized. Without evaluation, ideas and thought-starters fizzle and don't become solutions to the problems or issues.

First Aid for Feedback Evaluating Ideas:

- Learn to observe non-verbal feedback during the meeting, and respond accordingly.
- Separate creating ideas from evaluating ideas.
- Learn the language of positive feedback and how to give a balanced response when evaluating ideas and suggestions.
- Develop constructive ways to sort out and prioritize the best ideas.

Observe Feedback During the Meeting and Respond Accordingly

One thing that keeps meetings interesting, relevant and productive is for the facilitator and presenters to constantly monitor feedback from the group members and respond accordingly. This means observing body language, sleepy eyes, people looking out the window or reading unrelated material, and other clues that the group is not fully involved. I am amazed at how many speakers deliver a presentation without sensing and adjusting their delivery to respond to the feedback that people give so freely.

Responding to feedback can take many forms, from major interventions to subtle adjustments. For example, if it appears that the group doesn't understand complex information, the facilitator or presenter should check with participants to see if further explanation is needed. For example, ask members for their interpretation, or open up a discussion to the whole group. In this way, members will add more specific verbal feedback to their non-verbal signals. The result is that they will also stay focused on the topic.

Other techniques facilitators and presenters can use to respond to feedback are covered elsewhere in this book. These include calling a break, introducing a game or energizer, or changing the mode of presentation.

Separate Idea Generating from Evaluating

One of the basic principles of brainstorming established by Alex Osborn over a half-century ago is to separate the process of generating ideas from evaluating ideas. By generating ideas without first evaluating them, new ideas are given a chance to incubate and flourish. The longer ideas are kept alive, the more they begin to grow on people, to capture their imagination. Soon others begin to appreciate them and suggest ways to improve the ideas, by building and shaping them with ideas and "builds" of their own.

> Kelly had been quiet for much of the council meeting, which was centered on ways to re-energize the church's lagging capital funds campaign. She was the newest member of the group and was a naturally shy person. At one point, she asked, "What if we borrow the money from ourselves?"
>
> The recorder wrote "borrow from ourselves" on the flip chart along with all the other ideas. The council was in the midst of a free-flow of ideas, and this was one of many. A little later Fred said, "I'd like to return to the idea of borrowing from ourselves. What did you have in mind, Kelly?" Kelly explained her idea in more detail. She wondered if we could bypass the banks by asking church members to loan money directly to the church. Chuck said he remembered reading about a company that specialized in underwriting bond issues for churches but couldn't remember the details.

A week later the brochure from the bond under-writer was found and the firm contacted. Within three months the church completed a highly successful bond drive to raise the funds for the parish hall renovation. The bond issue sold out in less than a week, with church members buying the entire issue. Indeed, they borrowed the money from themselves, all because Kelly's idea was given a chance to grow and flourish. What would have happened if someone responded to Kelly by saying, "What are you, crazy? We're not millionaires!"

Separating idea generating from evaluating will greatly increase the number of ideas created. If your goal is to come up with three options for a problem, wouldn't you rather choose from dozens of alternatives than only a few? Original ideas or thought-starters may be partly developed concepts, or even totally unworkable, off-the-wall notions. By simply recording ideas without evaluating them as they occur, one thought sparks another and eventually workable solutions begin to emerge. This is when meetings become stimulating and fun!

Separating the two processes doesn't, however, mean ignoring the flaws in ideas. It simply means withholding judgment until lots of ideas from the group are on one table before switching into the evaluation mode.

Learn the Language of Positive Feedback and Balanced Responses

The effect of negative response is dramatic. Idea busters or killer phrases do more than squash a particular idea — they could send a message to group members that their ideas are not welcome, especially if the judgment comes from the boss or another senior person.

We are often not aware of how devastating our cynical judgments can be. The first step is for group members to increase their awareness of which answers crush ideas. Once a person becomes aware, it is not too difficult to learn new reactions that transform harsh impulses into words of encouragement. The following list compares judgments that crush ideas with language that builds ideas.

Instead of ...	Say ...
It just doesn't grab me.	Tell me more.
We tried that before and it didn't work.	What's different now, and what can we change to make it work?
It's been done to death.	Let's do it better (or differently).
We can't afford that.	How can we share budgets (find the money)?
Don't fight the system.	Let's change the system.
We've never done anything like that.	This breaks new ground.
The boss will never buy it.	How can we sell it to the boss?
That's really off the wall.	How could we test your idea?
Oh??	Yes! Let's try it.
I like my idea better.	Let's combine our ideas to get the best solution.
The timing isn't right.	Let's work out the best timing.

That only solves half the problem.	Let's isolate what works and then focus on the concerns.
We need something more exciting.	How can we add excitement?
Great idea, but not for us.	Great idea — how can we make it fit (work) for us?
Where'd you get that idea?	Bravo! Great thinking!
It'll never work (fly, sell).	How can we make it work (fly, sell)?
I have a better idea...	Building on your idea...
What will the board (committee) say?	Let's make sure we address the board's (committee's) concerns.
Yes, but...	Yes, and...
I don't agree.	I agree with (x and y) and need help in understanding (z).

Use the Balanced Response Technique

Many people erroneously think that evaluating ideas means exposing what is wrong with them. The problem with that common approach is that it often throws out the good with the bad. Few ideas are totally bad or worthless, and rarely are they perfect either, especially when first formulated. A more productive way to evaluate ideas (suggestions, concepts, etc.) is to identify and preserve the strengths while looking for a way to overcome the concerns. One technique to extract the "good stuff" from ideas and then find ways to make them work is the balanced response. This is based on answering with itemized responses, used in the synectics idea-generation technique.

Here's how it works: Identify at least three positive aspects of an idea or concept, such as its strengths, strategic fit, affordability, appeal, or whatever you like about it. Write these "pluses" on a flip chart (group notes). Then identify and write any concerns about the idea on the flip chart — describing a specific problem to be solved, using "how can we" or "I wish" language.

For an example of a balanced response, let's say a private school wants to explore using its classrooms during the summer. The challenge is stated as, "How to increase classroom use in the summer months." In a brainstorm meeting, one idea suggested is to air-condition the school. One way to respond to this idea (the usual) is to immediately exclaim why it won't work, such as, "That's absurd; it will cost a fortune!" When this happens, the idea is likely to be dropped, because some people will agree with the negative comment. However, using the balanced response technique to evaluate this idea, the positives are identified:

+   We could schedule adult education courses all summer long.
+   We could use classrooms for inter-generation summer camp activities.
+   Would benefit students (and teachers) in September and May to June.
+   We might be able to use the heating ducts, saving money.

Then the concerns are identified:

-   Affordability. (Written as: "How can we pay for it?")

Are adult education or other programs viable? ("I wish we knew...")

The balanced response forces the group to identify and isolate the suitable parts and then focus on the concerns — the parts that need work — describing each concern as a problem to be solved.

In the example, "How can we pay for it?" it becomes a new challenge or problem to be solved, causing the group to generate specific ideas. These might include:

- Hold fundraising events or a bond drive.
- Buy a reconditioned system.
- Find sponsors.

Addressing the second concern ("I wish we knew if programs were viable"), ideas might include:

- Run a test program during the fall.
- Send a questionnaire to probe interest to a sample of the community.

As the group works through issues that address the concerns, the original idea is transformed into a possible solution, ranked with other alternatives. Many concerns crop up in the area of implementation. For example, "That's a great idea, but where are we going to get the money?" By identifying and isolating the strengths of an idea, then focusing on the dilemmas, treating them as "how can we" rather than "we can't," any idea becomes possible until all avenues for improving it have been exhausted.

The balanced response refines many good ideas that might otherwise be lost so they can be examined and developed on their merits. People are empowered when their ideas are respected and developed. As we will discuss later, the balanced response is also a useful method to build consensus among group members.

Learn How to Sort Out and Prioritize Ideas

Building ideas using the balanced response or other techniques helps ensure that they are given a chance. The process does not stop there, however. Ideas must be sorted and prioritized so the group is able to choose the best solution.

Here are some methods that can be used to select and prioritize ideas:

- Dot Voting. Use this method when a large number of ideas are written on flip charts and hung around the room. All group members are given five to ten self-adhesive colored dots, to place next to ideas which they feel are best — either based on judgment or against specified criteria. At the end of the process, the winning ideas will be apparent to all; simply add up the ideas with the most dot votes, and rank them. Recognize that the dot voting method reflects only the input of the people voting. It does, however, provide a quick and fun way to get instant feedback from the group, and it virtually guarantees consensus, since everyone is voting the same way. Dot voting also may be done by groups asked to evaluate ideas generated by others.

- Quick Sort. This approach requires group members to sort all ideas into one of several categories in order to sort them. For example, categories might include: 1) Winners — implement immediately; 2) Terrific — find a way; 3) Incubate; and 4) Not now. Make up your own categories if you wish, but keep them positive. Imagine how you would feel if your idea was thrown into a category labeled "dogs." Remember that a certain idea might not be the answer for today's problem, but it might provide the pathway to another idea or solution tomorrow.

- Rate versus Criteria. After ideas have been whittled down to a manageable number, it is often useful to choose the "best of the best." Rating ideas against specific criteria is one way to do this. Criteria used should stem from the objectives and strategies you have established. For example, if the goal is to propose new product ideas for snack products targeted at teens, criteria might include: 1) Appeal to teens; 2) Technology available; 3) Innovative packaging; 4) Bring to market in one year; and 5) Offers competitive insulation. Alternative ideas or concepts may simply be checked off against these standards or rated on a 1-5 or 1-10 scale on how well they meet the criteria. A refinement of this method is to assign a point value to each of the criteria. Then rate the ideas on a 1-5 or 1-10 scale. Multiply the ratings times the point value and add up the results. See the example below:

Criteria	Value (1-10)	Idea 1 (Tot)	Idea 2 (Tot)	Idea 3 (Tot)
Appeal to teens	9	6 (54)	8 (72)	4 (36)
Technology available	7	4 (28)	6 (42)	9 (63)
Packaging	5	9 (45)	2 (10)	7 (35)
Market one year	6	2 (12)	8 (16)	6 (36)
Total rating		139	140	170

The value of methods such as Dot Voting, Quick Sort, and Rating versus Criteria is that each easily measures the consensus of the group. From this point, more evaluation or research might be needed to confirm the group's opinion.

8

Fun and Fellowship

"For the next two hours, we are going to ask that you resist your natural impulses to laugh out loud when something strikes you funny. In fact, even giggles and smirks will be looked on with disdain. We're about serious business here, and having fun is clearly inconsistent with our meeting purpose. Our goal is to generate some new approaches for reducing employee turnover. Now let's get going with some really creative ideas."

The Symptoms:

Taking Ourselves Too Seriously

If we could view videos of some of the meetings we have attended, I suspect many of us would grimace at how terribly pragmatic and serious they are. We might also notice that, whenever laughter broke out amidst the boredom, it often became a catalyst for relieving pressure and making progress in the group. Humor often helps us cut through the titles, the posturing, and the positions that limit our thinking and stifle participation.

Naturally, we should take our work seriously — it's what we get paid to do, or what we have agreed to do as a volunteer committee member. What happens all too often, however, is that we take ourselves too seriously. We get wrapped up in our self-importance and somehow think we have to always act seriously now that we have the title of manager, committee head, or project leader.

The result of all this seriousness often spills over into meetings. It seems "wrong" somehow to have fun when we are supposed to be working. So we stifle playfulness and laughter and instead hold boring, humorless meetings. When humor is used positively, most of us appreciate the lightness it brings to a meeting. Used properly, humor can enhance a meeting.

When presenting to the board of directors of American Brands, I wanted to convey that our foods division was innovative and forward thinking. We were prepared to defend a dramatic recommendation for reducing our product line from over four hundred items to about seventy, in order to concentrate on the best-selling, most profitable items. Since our plan would require a major write-off for inventory of discontinued items, it would be expensive. The night before the presentation, I was helping repair a few of my daughter's broken dolls and got an inspiration for a visual aid.

The presentation went well, and I purposely left out any reference to the cost. The chairman made some comments, took a puff on his cigar, and then asked what our plan would cost. I pulled out my visual aid, which was a poster with a doll's arm and a leg attached, from the spare parts box, of course. Holding up the visual, I looked the chairman straight in the eye and said, "Bob, it's not going to be cheap … it's going to cost you an arm and a leg!" The stunned board members were silent until the chairman cracked a little smile, which widened into a grin and then laughter. Soon, everyone appreciated not only my humor, but the boldness of our approach. The meeting turned into a lively discussion of the pros and cons of the proposal, with little regard to power, position, or any of the other barriers.

Is there a risk in using humor? I suppose I could have been fired for such an approach. Fortunately, I had done some research on "Chairman Bob" and discovered that he appreciated directness and a good laugh. Even with that information, I did not decide to use my audacious visual aid until I read the feedback from both the chairman and others. The risk was definitely worth it. And yes, the proposal was approved.

Not Enough Variety = Boring Meetings

We have mentioned ways in which potentially exciting meetings can become boring: unclear purpose, the wrong people in the meeting, lack of preparation, wandering from the agenda, and others. Another way to guarantee boredom is to limit the ways in which information is delivered or discussed. This means having one person talk too long, handling all agenda items in the same way, and using look-alike visual aids for all presentations.

Too much of anything is generally too much. For example, five to fifteen minutes of a well-produced video can bring life and zest to a meeting, while a two-hour video on any subject becomes boring at some point, no matter how well-produced. Because I have a short attention span, I am aware of my bias in this area. Nonetheless, I have seen many group members drift into "Never-Never Land" midway through a meeting, because there was not enough variety to keep them interested and involved.

Group Members Do Not Know Each Other

This symptom occurs in newly formed groups and in groups that do not normally meet together. I have also seen it happen in groups that have been meeting for months or years. There is a limit to the productivity of meetings if group members do not know each other on a personal level. When there is no disclosure or intimacy, people tend to talk at one another rather than with each other. While the type of group and purpose of the meeting determines the degree of familiarity, it usually enriches the meeting in many ways.

Other cultures value familiarity far more than North Americans, especially in Asian and Hispanic countries. Many American business people have learned the hard way that they need to invest time in building relationships with foreign business associates before charging into a fact-oriented, fast-paced presentation. Without knowing anything about the other people in a meeting, participants make assumptions as they attempt to discuss, collaborate, and make decisions.

First Aid for Boring Meetings:

- Lighten up, encourage humor and fun in your meetings.
- Use a number of different formats and techniques to inject fun and variety, and to keep things interesting.
- Use games, exercises and other means to enable group members to know one another better and build fellowship.

Lighten Up

Learn to include humor in your meetings. It can be as simple as starting out the meeting by asking participants to share something humorous that happened in their department, or showing the latest "Dilbert" cartoon. In Chapter 6, we noted that a useful skill for facilitators is a good sense of humor. There is, however, a distinction between humor and comedy. Professionals get paid to perform comedy, and they work hard at their material and delivery. Instead, what we're talking about is finding the humor in everyday situations, observing and reflecting on the absurdity of events, people and circumstances. Real life is usually funnier than prepared comedy material anyway. Have you noticed that comedy is usually derived from stories about real life, rather than contrived jokes or "shtick"?

Professional speakers and trainers have long known that wrapping serious messages around funny anecdotes not only makes a more interesting and palatable presentation, but it improves retention as well. Sharing funny stories about work-related subjects helps relax people and builds positive energy.

Be aware that it is possible for humor to backfire. Inappropriate humor can detract from an important discussion, or demean someone who is trying hard to understand something. And, like most things, too much humor is too much. Certainly, sarcasm and ethnic, racist or sexist jokes have no place in meetings. One healthy habit to nurture is the ability to laugh at yourself because, of course, humans are not perfect. Self-deprecating humor is especially refreshing from the boss.

Other ways to include fun in your meetings are games, energizers and exercises, many of which are covered in this chapter and in other parts of this book. Sometimes a simple humorous remark can break the ice and make a profound difference in the direction of a meeting.

My boss Jack and I were reviewing potential design firms to redesign the packaging graphics on several food products. A number of piecemeal changes had been made to the products over the years. While each change had probably been made for good reason, the line did not stand out among its competitors on grocery store shelves. In fact, the whole array resembled a patchwork quilt rather than a unified product line. Since Jack and I were both fairly new with the company, we carried none of the history and "baggage" of our predecessors. Instead, we were open to dramatic change, unlike our forerunners, who were reputed to be conservative about packaging designs.

During a meeting with one design firm, we noticed that there was a lot of posturing and hedging going on about the current line. This particular firm had done some of the previous work, and they were not sure if either of us had a vested interest in the present designs. At one point Jack, who was the vice president of marketing at our firm, interrupted and observed, "What you're really saying is that we have a screaming disaster here!" After gulping and looking at each other, the two representatives answered tentatively, "Well, yes." Then Jack and I smiled, everyone had a good laugh, and we finally started talking about the real issues and possible solutions in an open, candid manner.

Learn to laugh, and cultivate an environment that allows and encourages everyone to have fun while setting about the serious task of accomplishing your goals.

Use a Mixture of Formats and Techniques for Fun, Variety and Interest

Here are some ways to keep meetings lively, engaging and fun:

- Change some aspect of the meeting about every twenty minutes or so. Incorporate a mix of stimuli, such as solo presentations, group discussions, question-and-answer sessions, small group breakouts (see below), videos, panels, team presentations, individual and group idea generating, voting, exercises and games.
- Break a large group (more than eight) into smaller groups often for discussion, brainstorming and recommendations. Have each group report back to the larger group. This does not have to be done in separate rooms. In fact,

there is an advantage to holding "instant" breakouts in the large meeting room — the buzz and energy are stimulating.

- Hold a stand-up meeting. Few people will fall asleep, and the meeting will probably be much shorter. If the recorder takes notes on a flip chart, no one else has to. Many organizations schedule stand-up meetings with great success.

- Make visual aids graphic. Pictures, drawings, charts and graphs communicate many concepts quicker and more effectively than the spoken word.

- Change the meeting environment, just for the fun of it. Meet outside on a nice day, or hold a brunch meeting. Meet by fax and conference call.

- Change the media for visual support of presentations. Mix slides, overheads, videos, live props, computer visuals, handouts.

- Enroll people who make a lot of presentations in a hands-on course to improve their skills. The best ones are laboratory-type seminars that use video feedback to record practice presentations and coaching.

- Take two-minute stretch breaks to change the pace and recharge everyone. See Chapter 4 for more ideas about breaks.

- Use a process such as mindmapping — a visual tool to capture and express complex ideas — for exploring ideas, to process evaluation, and to enhance both self-expression and communication.

A good source of ideas is *Mindmapping: Your Personal Guide to Exploring Creativity and Problem-solving,* by Joyce Wycoff (Berkeley Publishing Group, 1992).

- Use brain-teasers (mental puzzles) at the beginning or anytime during a meeting to provide stimulation, a fun discourse and warm-ups for brainstorming. Two sources are listed at the end of this chapter.

- Start a meeting at an unusual time, such as 9:03, and promise the group that it will end promptly at 10:44. And then stick to those times.

- Have someone make a list of all the jargon used in a meeting, and then read it back to the group at the end. Ask yourselves what real people (or aliens) would think if they were a "fly on the wall" during such a meeting.

- Throw a Nerf™ ball or other soft object at anyone who criticizes or negates an idea during a brainstorming session. The person who has the ball can then throw it at the next naysayer. This is a harmless, fun way to reinforce the "idea generating before evaluating" ground rule.

Use Games and Exercises to Enhance Fun and Fellowship

In most areas of life, as soon as you learn more about a person, you begin to relate to him or her differently. If you learn that Bill spent fifteen years in engineering, you understand why and how he is able to come up with quick answers to highly technical challenges. When you learn of Stephanie's struggles raising four children, you appreciate her insights into your product's target market of young mothers. Knowing Bert's background in banking adds credibility to his comments on your board's quarterly financial statement.

Sharing personal information has value in any group. The extent to which group members disclose their histories depends partly on the type of group. Social organizations are at one end of the spectrum, while business groups obviously are at the other end. Before you dismiss the value of personal disclosure, consider trying it and see what happens in the group.

Games and exercises are a fun, non-threatening way to accomplish this. For example, in one church group we took a minute or two for each person to "check in" with the rest of the group, telling a little about what had brought joy or frustration since we last met. When facilitating idea-generating groups for any type of organization, one of the first things I do is have group members introduce themselves with some personal information, such as their favorite hobby or what they were known for in high school. When selecting methods to get to know one another, look for exercises that delve beyond jobs or titles to who the real person is, and how they think and act outside the work or organization.

One of my favorite ice-breaker exercises is "Two Truths and a Lie." Each person is asked to tell the group three facts about himself/herself that others probably wouldn't know. Everyone is asked to dig into their past or present and come up with something that will challenge the group. Examples: "I was a high school cheerleader." "My wife is a funeral director." "My passion is playing chess [or skiing, singing, making model airplanes]." "I collect rare coins."

Then the twist: One of the "facts" must be a lie. After the three facts are revealed, one person at a time, the other group members try to guess which one is the lie. The result is that group members learn some interesting information about each other ... and they also learn who is good at telling a lie! When everyone gets into the spirit, this is a fun exercise that gets the meeting off to a great start.

> In one meeting, we were in the midst of this exercise when a latecomer arrived. I asked him to make out a nametag and quickly explained what we were doing. When his turn came, we tried to guess which one of his statements was the lie. It turned out that none of them were lies ... all of the statements were true. Reading his nametag, I said, "Mark, what's the lie?" He replied, "My name is Stan, not Mark." Obviously, the group was off to a great start. Later, we used Stan's (a.k.a. Mark) example to make the point that sometimes you have to break the rules.

Here are some additional games and exercises you can use to break the ice and make it easy for people to share personal information.

- Have group members pair off and relate some personal history for a minute or so each. You might suggest specific questions, such as asking about their major in college, or favorite leisure activities. Then have each person introduce his/her partner, recounting as much information as they remember. This exercise also builds listening skills.

- Ask group members to imagine what they would do if they won the lottery and found themselves $20 million richer, and then describe their dreams. This reveals dreams, goals and motivations.

- Have group members draw their favorite animal when they were a kid, then share it in the large group, or with one other person.

- Ask group members, "Which actor [living or dead] would you choose to play you in a movie of your life?" and explain why.

- Start the meeting by having each person describe something at work or home that has been very satisfying, plus something that has been frustrating.

- Go around the room at the beginning of the meeting and ask each person what his/her expectations are for the meeting. Write these headlines on a flip chart sheet and post it. While this exercise reveals less-personal information, it is a good way for the leader, facilitator and other members to learn what each person expects to accomplish. This exercise works especially well in training sessions and in strategic planning meetings and retreats.

- Go around the room and have each person complete the sentence: "When I was seventeen..." This might be a recollection of memories from high school, summer jobs, being in love, or whatever comes to mind.

- Ask each person to identify his/her hero or heroine, and tell the group members why they admire that person. Similarly, invite group members to fantasize meeting one person whom they admire, then describe this dream meeting. To build on this, suggest that they would be able to ask this person one question — what would the question be?

- Ask each group member how life would be different if humans did not need to sleep. Ask each to further expand on how this would affect his/her life.

- Ask each to reflect on his/her best friend, and describe the qualities which make those friends special. Discuss your friendship with other group members in small or large groups.

These exercises, and many similar ones, can be done one-on-one, in groups of three or four, or in larger groups. Time may be a factor in deciding how to structure the exercise; for example, in a group of twenty people, a big chunk of time can be consumed if each person talks for two or three minutes. Get around this by breaking a larger group into subgroups (also known as "buzz groups") of three to six people.

In addition to games and exercises, consider allowing some unstructured social time before or after the meeting, or during a break. The more people know about each other, the better they will relate to each other in meetings. For longer meetings like conferences and retreats, an informal get-together the night before the meeting starts is a good way for participants to learn a little bit about each other. It will make a significant difference in the meeting the next day.

If you are in an organization with a training department, ask some of the trainers to describe some of the games and energizers they use to perk up training sessions. Many of these can be highly effective to liven up your meetings. *Games* magazine is an excellent source of brain-teasers and puzzles. Another treasure trove of games is *The Big Book of Business Games,* by Edward E. Scannell and John W. Newstrom, McGraw-Hill, 1996.

Recap of Part II

Planning a meeting provides the foundation for success. Working the plan makes the meeting flow. Implement the Four F's:

- *Focus* — Get everybody on board with the purpose, follow the prioritized agenda, record ideas on group notes, and manage time.
- *Facilitation* — Use a facilitator for each meeting, and encourage all participants to learn and use effective meeting skills.
- *Feedback* — Respond to ongoing feedback; learn constructive ways to evaluate ideas and build them into solutions.
- *Fun and Fellowship* — Lighten up your meetings with laughter and humor and get to know each other as people.

Part III

The Final Steps:
The Four C's of Completion

" There's a motion on the floor to call the Northside fire station...all in favor..."

The Final Steps:
The Four C's of Completion

9. Consensus

Make win/win decisions by consensus.

10. Closure

Establish clear action steps, timetables and responsibilities. End the meeting on time.

11. Critique and Celebration

Evaluate what was accomplished and the effectiveness of the process; affirm everyone's contribution.

12. Communication

Make a permanent record of the meeting results and distribute it to participants and others; then follow up to keep projects on track.

9

Consensus

- -

The truth you never hear:

"We've accomplished a great deal in our meeting today ... the group has generated tons of great ideas. I suppose it would be a good idea to get the group's opinion on which ones will work best. But instead, we'll just end the meeting now and leave everybody in the dark. I'll probably sit on these ideas for a few weeks, and then make the decision myself."

The Symptoms:

No Decisions Are Made

The meeting is winding down, and participants are congratulating themselves — deservedly so — after an intense session of generating ideas has produced several exciting alternatives. Many meetings end at this point, without committing to further action. Even if options and possible solutions have been evaluated for strengths and weaknesses and the most promising ones have been prioritized, nothing will happen until specific action decisions are made. These decisions outline which options will be implemented, researched further, or forwarded for approval — in other words, who will do what, by when.

There are many reasons why decisions do not get made. Perhaps there is no sense of urgency, or group members know that any "decision" they make is really only a recommendation, which ultimately has to be approved at a higher level. But the truth is, most task-oriented meetings cry out for decisions, yet most of us have attended meetings which have simply ended, with many things left undecided. Some meetings end with no decisions made, because it is clear that the boss — whether or not he/she is present — will finally make the decision(s) on the spot, or later, after the meeting is over.

Of course, making decisions is not always necessary at some types of meetings. The purpose of social meetings, motivational meetings, team-building, other training and meetings to give or receive information does not normally require the group to make decisions.

However, even social groups must decide when and where the next meeting will be held, the program or agenda, and who will be responsible for preparation and logistics. Simple as it sounds, many groups have difficulty making these types of decisions.

My wife and I were members of a church group that met every other week. Its purposes included fellowship, support and learning. The latter was most often accomplished by studying and discussing a book. The discussions were led by rotating group members.

Remembering this wonderful group, it's funny to realize just how much time we spent discussing the potential topics for study, and who would lead them. While such decisions were important, yet not really critical, we spent inordinate amounts of time on them. We finally made some headway when we devoted most of one meeting to planning programs and selecting leaders several weeks in advance.

Autocratic Decisions

It sometimes seems that autocratic decisions — those made solely by one person, usually the boss or committee head — have no place in enlightened organizations. For the most part, this is true. Certainly, it does not make sense to seek the ideas and opinions of others if one's mind is already made up.

In fact, there are many autocratic decisions, such as deciding to hire or fire someone or an entrepreneur's committing to personal risk. A leader is perfectly within his/her rights to hold a meeting where group members generate ideas, review and analyze options, but then do not make decisions. Sometimes the leader makes the decision later, after mulling over the input from the group. The risk of this approach, however, is that there will be little or no support from the group for the ultimate decision if they did not participate in the decision-making process.

If you call a meeting to get ideas or feedback, it is important to be very clear about your intentions. For example, if you solicit ideas, suggestions or feedback from employees, let the participants know how the information will be processed and used — how, when and by whom decisions will be made and action taken. If you gather candid feedback and ideas from employees, you are then compelled to take whatever action is necessary. Otherwise, the whole process might backfire.

A large telephone mail-order center asked me to facilitate a series of employee focus group meetings. The purpose was to get input for the human resources department and top management for structuring employee benefits, and to understand employee attitudes toward the company.

During these meetings, I noticed a lot of resentment from employees toward their supervisors and managers. Many were hesitant about participating in a session of this type, fearing that any negative comments might be used against them, although I was an outside contractor. I assured participants of their anonymity and was able to elicit some useful information. Still, some group members were skeptical that management would take action on their suggestions.

As it turned out, little concrete action was taken as a result of the focus group meetings, which ultimately confirmed the employees' suspicions. I often wonder why they invested the time and money to gather the feedback if they never intended to act on the results.

Win/Lose Decisions

Decisions are made in all kinds of groups by win/lose voting. Even though voting is better than making no decisions, it is often not the best way to keep all group members "whole" and totally committed to the outcome. Why? The simple act of voting on decisions sets up a win/lose situation. Those who vote with the majority "win," and those who do not "lose." It seems fair; after all, it is the democratic process. Robert's Rules of Order, parliamentary procedure, and its many variations have led us to believe that majority voting is the best way to make a decision in a group. All in favor?

Here's the rub: nobody really likes to lose, no matter how close the vote. As a result, the "losers" — even if only a few people — may try to undermine the group decision, perhaps with others who did not attend the meeting. Those who did not vote with the majority may have unresolved issues and, if so, probably will not support the outcome. Depending on how close the vote and the emotional intensity, win/lose decisions could split the group and cause permanent damage to its effectiveness.

Groupthink

The meeting is going well. Almost immediately after the major problem is identified, the boss suggests a solution. Most group members quickly agree that it is a great idea, an obvious solution. Yet several aspects of the idea strike Georgeanne as impractical based on her experience. However, she chooses not to rock the boat. As a result, little discussion takes place, and the decision is made. Several weeks after it is carried out, fatal flaws are found that prove to be very costly. Welcome to the syndrome of groupthink.

First Aid for Decisions and Groupthink:

- Make win/win decisions by consensus.
- Avoid groupthink with diversity and time.

Make Win/Win Decisions by Consensus

Being able to reach consensus is the sign of a highly functioning group. Reaching consensus takes a little longer — at least initially — since it requires all group members to fully participate. The results are almost always worth it, because an effective group generates more options, evaluates alternatives more realistically, and selects the optimum solution(s) more than any one person can.

The big benefit to consensus decisions is that everybody wins: decisions are mutually beneficial and everyone feels good about them. There is usually a deeper commitment among group members to act on consensus decisions. Everyone's input has been heard, all contributions have been fully considered, and each feels the decision is the best of all the possible solutions. On the other hand, in win/lose decisions (e.g., majority vote), the losers are obliged to "go along" with the majority. Participants in a consensus process are fully invested in the decision, causing commitment and enthusiasm.

How does a group reach consensus anyway? More than most meeting skills, building consensus seems to be one of the most "mysterious" and least-understood processes. It doesn't have to be. In fact, consensus decisions flow directly from practicing the planning and flow skills already mentioned in this book. Consensus does not just happen; it evolves. Every time a group member or facilitator summarizes agreements or checks to make sure all concerns have been expressed, consensus is being built. Groups that reach consensus have these characteristics:

- Every participant is encouraged to contribute fully (see chapters 6 and 7). This means group members feel safe offering ideas and thought-starters, although they may not be fully developed, and are invited to build on others' contributions, making them as strong as possible.

- Points of agreement are frequently summarized (see chapters 5 and 6). The facilitator or another group member takes time out to summarize the group's progress and identify areas of agreement, along with areas for concern or further problem-solving.
- The strengths and concerns of a possible solution or course of action are expressed. Group members are encouraged to voice their concerns, no matter how big or small, without fear of attack from the leader or other members. The balanced response technique explained in Chapter 7 is a powerful tool for making this happen in a meeting.
- A possible solution with "flaws" is worked on and modified by the group until each member feels good about it, and no one feels he/she is giving up anything important.

At some point, it becomes obvious that the group has arrived at an acceptable solution, representing the best thinking of everyone included. The positive aspects are strong, and the problems have either been addressed or are acceptable to all. It is the facilitator's job to recognize this crucial point and to check out his or her conclusion with the group. Here are examples of language to test consensus:

"Let's see where we stand on [issue]. I think we all agree on [xyz]. Are there any more concerns?"

"How are we doing on this? Is there anything in [the proposal or solution] that you can't live with?"

"Let's take a straw vote here to get a sense of how close we are to a solution. Are you feeling pretty comfortable with what we are recommending?" (A straw vote is very informal. You don't even have to raise hands; just look for head nods, and probe group members whose body language lets you know there may be concerns.)

"I am sensing we are in general agreement ... is everyone comfortable with the recommendation as it stands?"

"Unless there are concerns we need to address, let's move forward..."

"Let's check out how close we are to a solution."

An important distinction must be made: consensus does not mean compromise. The idea of compromise means that someone gives up something important in order to reach an agreement. Consensus means that every person is comfortable with the decision (idea, recommendation, etc.), believing it is the best possible course of action for the group to take. No one has to "give up" anything.

The dynamics of consensus building embrace everything *First Aid for Meetings* is all about: meeting on purpose, good planning, having the right people, focus, facilitation, feedback, and fun. Group consensus is the natural outcome if everything else works. It requires group members to honestly express opinions and concerns, and to be open to suggestions and ideas for addressing them. Consensus also requires an attentive facilitator to know when to test the waters and call for closure on an issue or solution.

Avoid Groupthink

Beware of "groupthink" when trying to build consensus. Groupthink usually happens when one or a few vocal members are highly persuasive or assertively push for their ideas and points of view. In this situation, it becomes intimidating for less-expressive people to voice their concerns. As a result, they may "cave in" and go along with the group.

Groupthink can also happen when group members are insulated from the realities of the organization, such as boards or executive committees who are not in touch with what is happening at the operating level. This "emperor's new clothes" version of groupthink is reinforced when underlings are too intimidated by their superiors to question their decisions or point out their flaws.

"Groupthink" was first coined by psychologist Irving L. Janis, and it can also occur in groups that have been meeting over time and do not explore diverse viewpoints. Long meetings can also produce groupthink; everyone wants to go home, so decisions are rushed. Similarly, when groups are under pressure to make a decision, members don't use their usual assessment criteria, for the sake of group harmony. The risk of groupthink is that the best solutions are not found because of the lack of critical evaluation — all points of view are not heard.

To avoid groupthink, remember the following:

- Welcome diversity in your group. Invite people from other departments, those who are known to have different viewpoints from your own, and people who will be affected by the decisions your group makes.
- The leader (boss, committee head) sets the tone for divergent viewpoints. Participants must feel safe in expressing their reservations, instead of just parroting what the boss wants to hear.
- If a decision feels uncomfortable, delay the final decision-making until everyone has a chance to think it over. This also allows time for more research or data-gathering to support the decision.
- Seek the opinion of others in the organization before making a final decision. Tell them what you are considering, and why you think it will work. Listen carefully for input and suggestions to make your proposal stronger.

10

Closure

The truth you never hear:

"Well, we've stumbled along for over three hours, and we're almost done with the agenda. I hope somebody picks up the ball on all this stuff, because there's a lot to do if we're going to meet our deadline. I wonder what should we do with the items we weren't able to cover ... maybe they will just go away."

The Symptoms:

No Action/Fuzzy Action Steps

Most decisions are not an end; rather, they are part of a process of getting something done, solving problems, or developing and implementing a plan. Decisions require action: somebody must do something as a result. The action could be relatively easy, such as notifying other people; or more complex, such as initiating a research project. When action steps are not clearly spelled out, problems inevitably occur.

The scenario goes something like this: Janelle believes that Dick is going to write the report, while Dick assumes that Sylvia will do it, since she wrote the last one. Sylvia is busy on other projects and has no intention of taking action. As a result, the ball is dropped and nothing gets done. When it is time for accountability, there are plenty of puzzled looks ("I assumed...") and yet little has been done.

Action steps are a must.

Meetings Do Not End on Time

While this subject could easily fit in several sections of the book, ending a meeting on time is one of the most important actions a group can take to preserve commitment and enthusiasm. "Endless meetings syndrome" causes frustration, discomfort and anger in groups of all kinds. Few people appreciate meetings that drag on too long, especially if it "just happens" without group members agreeing to it.

Leaders who allow meetings to go overtime without negotiation assume that group members have nothing better to do with their time than to stay in the meeting. This ignores the fact that most people would rather speak for themselves regarding their time commitments. A scheduled one-hour meeting is not a license to hold people captive all morning or afternoon!

My experience, confirmed by informal research, indicates that lengthy meetings are a major frustration for people in organizations of all kinds. Many people have confided that lengthy, drawn-out meetings are a primary reason that they do not volunteer for committees, boards and task groups. In businesses, although employees might not have a choice whether or not to attend a meeting, their time is still valuable. In volunteer groups, the problem can undermine how they accomplish their goals.

First Aid for Open-ended Meetings:

- Assign specific action steps before the meeting ends: what will be done, who will do it, and when it will be done.
- End the meeting on time, or renegotiate the time contract with participants.

Assign Specific Action Steps

Most decisions will just sit there until somebody actually does something. Action is required. Action steps have three components:

- What has to be done?
  The "what" should be specific, so that there will be no misunderstanding by any group member or recipient regarding the action to be taken. Examples: additional research, get approvals to decisions/recommendations, request funds, write a proposal or presentation, hire more people, or start a project.
- When must it be done?
  This simply means laying out the timetable for checkpoints and completion of the action. Include key dates, and describe how they will be monitored.

- Who will do it?
  Before ending the meeting, assign specific responsibility for all action steps. This means asking for volunteers or assigning the action steps to individuals or committees, who agree to complete it by the timetable indicated.

Examples of Action Steps:

- Joan will write the proposal asking for additional consumer research by Friday, March 3. Sanders will review and forward it for approval by Monday, March 6.
- Heather, Yvonne and Eric will review the group's ideas for new vendor guidelines by Tuesday, August 4, and send a copy of their proposal to all team members.
- All committee members will make a minimum of six telephone calls to church members to get their feedback on the capital campaign. Dottie will provide the list of names, and calls are to be completed by November 15.
- Peg will research the latest models of telephone-answering machines in our price range, and report back at the next meeting.
- Nell and Barry will make engineering drawings of the three top ideas for a fuel transport system and forward them to the vice-president of engineering for review by November 15.

As action items come up during the meeting, it's a good idea to have the recorder write them down or note them in some special way (special mark on the flip chart, or highlight if recording on computer). Toward the end of the meeting, the recorder or facilitator should review all action items, and add new action items for any project or issue that requires follow-up.

Many groups get stuck on assigning the "who will do it" part of action items. Often people are reluctant to bring up ideas, because they fear they'll get saddled with doing the work. What a shame! In virtually every group, some people are better at coming up with ideas, and others are more adept at follow-through and implementation. In fact, you could be inviting disappointment if you assign a good "generator" the responsibility for detailed follow-through. When a meeting is focused on gathering ideas, the person(s) best suited for action and follow-through might not be obvious. Solution? Allow people to volunteer for action steps. Make it clear at the outset that both skills are critical to successful projects.

End Meetings on Time

Most group members are all smiles when a meeting ends early; many people are astonished that it could even happen! It can. There are several ways to do it.

One method is to come to an abrupt stop at the agreed-upon ending time, no matter what. This dramatic approach is not recommended, because there is likely to be unfinished business, which creates other frustrations and problems.

A modified approach to an abrupt stop is to monitor the time throughout the meeting, using the timekeeper. For example, a time check could be given every half-hour, or at the end of each time segment scheduled for the agenda items. After each time reminder, the facilitator can briefly summarize what has been covered, and highlight what is left on the agenda. During the final ten to fifteen minutes, the timekeeper reminds the group that time is almost up. The facilitator then asks the members how they would like to spend the last few minutes of the meeting.

Remember to save enough time for all business to be covered, including "parking lot" items, assigning action steps, assessing the meeting and deciding details of the next meeting. These minor issues can easily take fifteen minutes or more, after the meeting is supposedly over.

Manage Individual Meeting Segments

Managing individual meeting segments (or "meetings within the meeting") is another useful technique for ending on time and getting the most important things covered. If you have already planned the time required for each meeting topic, all you have to do is decide how to manage the time allocated to that topic.

For example, say you have allocated forty minutes to discuss a new personnel policy. The facilitator might suggest that the group spend the first ten minutes in a free-wheeling discussion, the next ten minutes isolating the most important problems or issues that emerge, and the next fifteen minutes generating ideas and selecting the best solutions. The last five minutes would be devoted to assigning action steps. Not all meeting topics need to be micro-managed to this extent — just the most important ones, where the potential for getting sidetracked and rambling discussions is high. Remember to use the "parking lot" idea for side issues.

Renegotiating the Time Contract

If you are near the end of the agreed-on meeting time, and it is clear some important issues will not be finished, the leader (with the facilitator's help) can renegotiate when to end with group members. Renegotiating can be a simple request, like, "I'd like to get everyone's input on this before tomorrow's management conference. Will you agree to extending our meeting another fifteen minutes?" Sometimes extending a meeting (or portion of a meeting that is part of a longer conference or retreat) can be very productive. If the group is on a roll, the extended time can create a sense of urgency to focus toward completion. However, remember that extending meetings, even with the agreement of all members, should be done sparingly. Extensions should always be for specific time periods (say, ten minutes), rather than open-ended.

One of the least-effective things groups can do when time is up is to simply forge ahead without comment. This does not respect participants' valuable time, regardless of their relationship to the group or the leader.

If the group decides to end the meeting, something must be done with remaining agenda items and "parking lot" issues, if any. The facilitator may suggest that the group carry them over until the next meeting, or that the items be handled in some other way, such as assigning them to individuals for study or action. If the issues are important, a separate meeting may be scheduled, with only the affected people attending.

11

Critique and Celebration

The truth you never hear:

"Bob, you were your usual obnoxious, over-bearing self in our meeting today. Not only did you ramble off in a thousand directions, you used your sick humor to offend several people. Furthermore, you interrupted just about everybody. Now, for the rest of you..."

The Symptoms:

Not Assessing Meeting or Group Effectiveness

You had a great meeting. Energy was high, the focus was clear, and many breakthrough ideas were generated. The group came to consensus decisions on the key issues. Action steps were assigned. The meeting started and ended on time. Everyone attending agreed it was one of the best meetings they had ever attended.

Two weeks later the same group met to focus on additional problems facing the organization. Things were different from the very beginning, however. The energy level was lower. Several group members launched into unrelated topics that made the meeting lose focus several times. The hardest part was trying to decide on a course of action. The meeting ran overtime, with many loose ends unresolved. Everyone agreed it was one of the worst meetings they ever attended.

What made the first meeting work so well and the second meeting with the same group fail so miserably? Without any more information than is given, it is hard to tell. But a closer look shows that one problem with both meetings is that the group did not spend any time assessing what worked well and what could be improved. Without this appraisal, the group will never really know how to make — or keep — meetings more effective, except by chance.

Individual or Group Contributions Go Unrecognized

Normally, Marianne was quiet in committee meetings. This time, however, things were different. It was clear that Marianne had spent extra time and energy to gather information on how to recruit more volunteers for the group's major fundraiser. She had done extra research and consulted experts, and consequently her ideas were fresh, strategically sound, and well thought out.

Unfortunately, several important items were on the committee's agenda the day Marianne offered her ideas, and her efforts went unrecognized. The fundraising program seemed lost in the many other issues discussed by the group. As a result, no one acknowledged Marianne for her extra efforts, and the ideas were not processed by the group. As you might expect, for the next few meetings Marianne retreated to her "quiet mode" once again and contributed only minimally to the topics under discussion.

Some groups are so task oriented and serious that they concentrate solely on the work at hand. Many leaders and facilitators fail to appreciate the power of recognizing and affirming people for their contributions, both individually and for the group as a whole.

First Aid for Assessing Meetings and Recognizing People:

- Take time to critique each meeting, identifying what worked and what could be improved. Consider using a process observer.
- Notice, reward and celebrate individual and group contributions.

Critique Each Meeting

It is highly productive to take a few minutes at the end of every meeting to identify:

- What occurred in the meeting that worked. This includes identifying techniques used by group members or the facilitator to stay on task, or to build cohesiveness (Chapter Six).
- What could be changed or accomplished differently to make the meeting even more effective. This would include observations of disruptive or non-productive behaviors (focusing on the

behavior, not the people involved), time
management, and preparation.

Once a group gets the hang of it, assessing can be
done in a few minutes or less. Beware of over-generalizing.
There is a tendency to think that everything went well in an
effective meeting and that everything went wrong in a
meeting that is generally boring or non-productive. The
reality is that, in every meeting, some things work and some
things do not. The balanced response (Chapter Seven)
works well as a tool for assessing meetings.

At the end of a recent planning conference, the
facilitator asked each participant to jot down at least
three things that worked well in the meeting, and up
to three things that they would change to make the
meeting more effective. The comments could relate
to things done to accomplish the purpose (task) or
maintain group harmony and cohesiveness, and were
to be as specific as possible. She then asked each
person to pick one from each column and read it
aloud to the group. The interchange was both lively
and informative and helped make this group's phone
conferences even more effective.

Here are some of the responses:

Things That Worked ...	*What We Could Improve ...*
John credited Elysse, and built on her ideas for publicity.	Start the meeting on time, without waiting for latecomers.
Had agenda in advance, with chance to update at beginning.	Limit discussion on items so everyone gets a chance to comment.
Stuck to agenda pretty well.	Come better prepared.
Summarized results at the end.	Establish a ground rule for side conversations.

Each person handed in comments, and the complete results were summarized and distributed to participants along with the minutes.

Critiquing a meeting in this way provides guidance for leaders, facilitators and participants. Using the balanced response reinforces skills and behaviors, and clarifies what can be improved can be used to set goals. Starting the next meeting with a capsule summary of what worked/what needs improvement sets a tone for a highly effective meeting.

Consider appointing a process observer as an alternative to having everyone debrief, which can take up valuable time with a large group. The process observer, who may also be a participant, is charged with observing, on behalf of the group, behaviors and skills that contribute to and detract from the meeting's success. At the end of the meeting, the observer gives a headline report on what was observed. By rotating this task, each participant will become more aware of meeting process skills.

For groups that meet frequently, such as committees, staff groups and teams, a more comprehensive evaluation is useful from time to time. Have each meeting participant fill out an evaluation, and have the results summarized and distributed. (Sample evaluation forms are in the Appendix.)

Celebrate Individual and Group Contributions

Leaders, facilitators and group members who take the time to recognize individual and group efforts are paving the way for enthusiastic participation and more effective meetings. Psychologists understand that behavior that is rewarded gets repeated — the more people are recognized for things they do to improve meetings, the more they are likely to repeat these positive behaviors. This can be especially helpful in groups that are just learning about the skills for running effective meetings.

Recognitions and celebrations do not have to be long and drawn out; a simple observation often works just as well. Examples:

> "Janet, your research was very helpful to our understanding of the extent of the problem. I especially like the way you summarized it for us."

> "Bill, when you suggested we all go around and give our opinion of the new personnel policy, it really helped us focus and get everyone's point of view."

> "When Allen told us how his people tried to implement the new voicemail system, I thought I'd die laughing. It really helped us all understand the work we have to do."

> "Rosita's observation that we were all too close to the situation to be objective was right on target. After we gather some customer comments, we will be in a better position to understand how our system really works. Thanks, Rosita."

Spontaneous applause for individuals, breakout teams, or the entire group is a powerful way to show appreciation. All it takes is for one person (the facilitator or anyone else) to start, and the rest of the group will join in. Think of a time when you were applauded for something you did. How did it make you feel? You can give that same gift to anyone who deserves it.

Positive feedback can be made anytime during the meeting. Encourage participants to identify and bring up positive contributions as they occur and again at the end of the meeting. It is better to save negative feedback (things that can be improved) until the end of the meeting, when it is least disruptive. In doing so, remember to use the balanced response, recapping the positive comments (what worked) first before diving into the concerns/things to improve.

After an especially productive meeting, why not do something special to celebrate? Here are some suggestions:

- As the leader, write all participants a personal thank-you note for their contributions to a great meeting.
- Order in pizza and beverages at the end of the meeting and celebrate with an instant party.
- Have every participant write down one thing that made the meeting work so well. Put these on self-adhesive notes and create a group montage.
- Similarly, have group members create a "guide-lines for great meetings" drawing or list, and post it in the meeting room. This list can also serve as meeting ground rules and can be modified as needed.
- Plan an off-site social event to celebrate the group's success. Such an outing will also allow group members the opportunity to get to know one another better in a relaxed setting.
- During longer retreats, consider cutting short scheduled work sessions as a reward for good work early on. This could be established at the beginning of the conference; maybe one afternoon work session would convert to free time if the work gets done in the early sessions.
- Say "thank you" often.

12

Communication

The needless statement you hear all too often:

"Ellen, did you second the motion to repair the water fountain, or was it Virginia? And who was it that suggested we meet every other week during the summer months? Was that made into a motion? Let me read the exact wording back to you to make sure it is right."

The Symptoms:

No Record of the Meeting is Kept

Many groups, especially those that meet together often, neither keep nor publish any record of their meetings. This is fine for some groups, such as social or study groups. For task-oriented groups, however, this can cause problems. In my experience, having no record of the meeting works only if each group member is disciplined to record his/her action steps and there is a high trust level. If things are not written down, people tend to forget (or selectively remember) commitments, action steps and timetables. Worse, good ideas that are not recorded may be lost forever. I have also observed groups where someone, such as the secretary or recorder, takes notes or minutes but does not distribute them to group members. What's the point?

Several years ago, I was on the publicity committee for our community theater group. We had a committee of six highly creative people, and at one meeting we came up with dozens of great ideas for getting the word out about our upcoming theater season. However, the ideas were not recorded, and at the end of an hour two of us had to leave. Afterwards, there was no feedback about the ideas, nor was any attempt made to summarize and decide the best ideas. The chairperson thanked everybody and said she would take care of the publicity. When the publicity program was launched, it seemed to miss the mark. Sadly, the group had come up with ideas that would have solved some of the problems we experienced. Many of us thought that the best ideas never saw the light of day. If a summary of the ideas had been prepared and sent to the committee participants, we might have been able to rescue the plan.

Minutes of the Meeting
Are Needlessly Detailed

The exact and perfect minutes from the group's secretary nearly drove the other group members crazy. Virtually every phrase uttered in the meeting was noted, and certainly every motion was rendered in precise language, including who made it, who seconded it, and how many voted yea or nay. In fact, the secretary interrupted the meeting flow several times to clarify who said what.

It was difficult to read the published minutes — everything that happened was there in exquisite detail. Because of the level of detail, group members seldom took the time to plow through them, and those who bothered often missed important items. For example, many action steps were missed because they were buried so deeply in the minutes. At the beginning of each meeting, the minutes from the previous meeting were approved. This process consumed valuable time because of the pointless detail. In fact, few people read the minutes before the meeting because they were so lengthy and dense.

Assuming Things Will Happen
Without Reminders

It would be great if our memories were perfect and our priorities always in sync so that we always finish the most important things first. In this ideal state, we would follow up on projects and work assignments in a timely fashion. We would be totally prepared for each meeting we attend and ready to report on items for which we are responsible. Does this sound like utopia? Unfortunately, for most of us, it is. We are human. Our lives are filled to overflowing with dozens of priorities related to work, family, friends, clubs, church, and recreation.

It is not wise to assume that because someone takes responsibility for an action item, and receives a reminder in the meeting summary, that it will get done. How many times have you been disappointed to learn that a project you assumed was finished hadn't even been started? While lack of follow-through can be a problem in businesses, it is also critical in organizations and boards which depend on volunteers to get the work done. The time to solve follow-through problems is before the next meeting.

First Aid for Follow-up:

- Using the group notes as a guide, prepare a brief written summary of major discussion items, action steps, timetables, and the people responsible.
- Send the summary to all attendees — and others who need to know — as soon as possible following the meeting.
- Establish a ground rule for accountability in your group.
- Start a follow-up system to periodically check on the progress of projects and timetables.

Prepare a Summary

Group notes are a powerful technique for posting the agenda, and recording ideas and decisions made during the meeting. The recorder writes ideas, key topics, and discussion points — in headline form — on a flip chart (or computer with a display) so all group members can see the ongoing output. While group notes are valuable during the meeting to keep focused, they also provide the raw material for writing a meeting summary.

The summary should include: 1) a recap of the main discussions; 2) decisions made; 3) action steps: what will be done, by whom and when; and 4) meeting process debriefing. An ideal meeting summary is no more than one page long. Here are two samples:

Benefits Task Force

Team Meeting held 11/12/96 at 2:30 p.m. — Main Conference Room

Attending: Suzie B., Tye C., Grace H., Lenny W., Jennifer C., Cate D.

Summary of Discussions:

1. 401-K Plan:
   a. After discussion, agreed that individual contributors could direct their plan funds into an expanded list of alternatives. ACTION: Tye to investigate details with broker and give report next meeting.
2. Vacation Policy:
   a. Response to employee survey strongly supported floating holiday concept. Agreed to offer it beginning 1/1/97 to all employees. ACTION: Suzie to present to Operating Committee.
   b. Grace presented results of informal inquiry of other local companies — our current policy (one-week vacation after one year's employment) was out of line. Group agreed to recommend modifying to one-week vacation after six months, two weeks after one year. ACTION: Grace to draw up and present to Operating Committee.
3. Stock Purchase Plan:
   a. Agreed to allow any employee to purchase shares of company stock with no commission directly through the treasurer's office. ACTION: Lenny to talk to treasurer.
   b. The brochure explaining this program should remind potential participants that this should be considered a long-term investment; short-term market fluctuations are likely to happen, given the recent history of the NASDAQ. ACTION: Jennifer to incorporate into the flyer.
4. Brainstorming — ideas group felt had great merit for further development:
   a. Offer long-term confidential financial planning at no cost to employees with over five years' service and for new hires at the department head and higher level.
   b. Mentor program: each employee would have a mentor for the first two years.
   c. Convert the old garage into an employee fitness center, open to all, including families.
   d. Training in general communications skills: writing, speaking, running meetings, etc., will be made available to employees who complete one year's service.

Action: Suzie to develop above ideas further, including costs, and report to group next meeting.

5. "Parking Lot" items: Birthday as holiday — handled by new floating holiday policy. Personalized mug for coffee break area — no action now.
6. Meeting process debrief: Started ten minutes late, but made up with Tye's good facilitation. Had to remind group about ground rules for brainstorming/idea generation; used "parking lot" concept for first time with good results. We only had two side conversations — good progress.
7. Next meeting: Mid-December, date to be determined. Please note your Action items.

First Church Board Meeting

Monthly Meeting held 6/2/96 at 7:00 p.m.

Attending: D. Crandall, C. Harris, L. Herbert, K. Norman, P. MacIvers,
H. Pancero, F. Wilder

Summary of Discussions:

1. Grounds and Maintenance Projects:
   a. Staining of church entrance and tile — target completion end of June 1996. K. Norman responsible.
   b. General church workday scheduled for 7/15; D. Crandall is in charge of rounding up volunteers by 7/10.
2. Fellowship:
   a. Pastoral Care committee will coordinate activities to follow up on people who have not attended in a while. Report on progress next board meeting. P. MacIvers in charge.
3. Adult Education:
   a. The current adult education series has been successful and will conclude in June. H. Pancero will survey members for topics for next fall and beyond. Survey to go out in the July newsletter.
4. Administration:
   a. C. Harris recommended that a separate committee be established to study revising the church bylaws. Agreed by consensus.
5. Finance: Our monthly obligation to repay the mortgage is now $3,325, as a result of refinancing.
6. "Parking Lot" items: All-church late fall event — all agreed it was a good idea; D. Harris to solicit ideas from board at next meeting. Come prepared!
7. Meeting process debrief: Everyone was well prepared on the financial situation because of L. Herbert's advance letter sent to board members. We need to do better at starting as early as possible following the morning service.
8. Next meeting: Sunday, August 25, 1996, following the 9:00 service. Be prepared to talk about plans, programs and events in your area as we gear up for the fall season.

To further reinforce and remind the members, the recorder or whoever sends out the summary can use a felt-tip pen to highlight each member's copy with action steps and follow-up.

If your group has difficulty weaning away from highly detailed minutes, examine the minutes or summaries from several previous meetings. How important or useful are explicit notes about who said what, who made and seconded motions, etc.? How is such information used? How does it serve the purpose of the group? If the only answer to any of these questions is, "We've always done it that way," or, "It's in our by-laws," consider changing the procedure, the by-laws or both, and move to preparing concise meeting summaries.

Send the Summary to People Who Need to Know

Preparing a summary will not accomplish much if participants and others do not receive it in a timely manner. Once completed, the meeting summary should be sent to:

1. People who attended the meeting, highlighting action steps on individual copies.
2. Group members and other interested people who did not attend the meeting.

The summary should be sent as soon as possible after the meeting, ideally within twenty-four hours. This will remind people of action steps while the "news" is still fresh and allow any incorrect information to be changed if needed.

If the meeting summary isn't distributed soon after the meeting, it may get lost in the clutter of other priorities, or among notes from three other meetings.

Once the recorder sends out the meeting summary, it is then the responsibility of all recipients to read it thoroughly, and to act on items for which they are responsible. Some groups send the summary to all attendees before sending copies to those not attending, to allow for any changes or corrections.

One of the least productive habits is to hand out the previous meeting's summary at the beginning of the following meeting. By then, it may be too late to take action, and reviewing the minutes consumes valuable meeting time.

Establish a Ground Rule for Accountability

When groups are first forming and members are trying to figure out their level of commitment and involvement, it is useful to establish a ground rule for accountability. In its simplest form, it means that group members commit to doing what they say they will do.

In ongoing groups, if there is no problem with follow-through, you may not need to address this issue. However, if some members are weak in follow-through on action items, accountability should be addressed as a group standard to which all members agree. The process of agreeing to this ground rule with other group members serves to remind everyone that commitments are taken seriously.

Start a Follow-up System

A follow-up system is like an insurance policy. It helps ensure that actions are taken and projects stay on track. Depending on the group, the person responsible for follow-up can be the group/meeting leader, facilitator or recorder. Follow-up may also be delegated to someone who did not attend the meeting, such as an administrative assistant. Follow-up reminders don't have to be heavy-handed; often a quick note is all that is needed.

On more complex projects, it's a good idea for the group or project leader to get more involved by checking with people directly between meetings, and offering help if needed. A good follow-up system helps minimize surprises at your next meeting.

Here are some follow-up options to consider; use whatever works for you or develop your own system.

- E-mail, fax or post card reminders:

"Edwina, your analysis of survey results is due at our next staff meeting. Let me know if you need any help in completing this."

"Looking forward to your report on membership at the February 12 conference. If you run into any snags in getting it done, Cas said he might be able to lend a hand. Give him or me a call if you need help."

- Send out a copy of the meeting summary high-lighting the action step(s), perhaps with a hand-written note:

"You really wowed us last meeting — we are all excited about your next report. Thanks for your insightful contributions."

- Pick up the phone and call the person:

"Hi, Carol, this is Josh. Just checking over the notes from last meeting and wanted to make sure you were on track for the budget presentation a week from now."

In every follow-up communication, leave the door open for people to ask for help if they need it. There may be dozens of legitimate reasons why something is not done or falls behind schedule, and the time to find out about it is before the next meeting. If you stay in touch with the responsible members, you can give input or assistance, assign the project to someone else, or do it yourself if they run into difficulties.

With a solid follow-up and accountability system, the meeting process comes full circle. Action steps and follow-up are a critical part of the preparation for the group's next meeting.

Recap of Part III

Most meetings are not over when the group leaves the room. Understanding that meetings are held to accomplish specific purposes, the discussions and decisions almost always require action and follow-up of some kind. In addition, the only way for a group to improve its meeting effectiveness is to properly assess things that work and what can be improved. Remember the Four C's:

- Consensus — Arrive at win/win solutions and decisions by consensus.
- Closure — Establish clear action steps, timetables and responsibilities; end on time.
- Critique and Celebration — Assess the meeting effectiveness and acknowledge the contributions of those who made it work.
- Communication — Prepare a concise summary of the output and distribute it as soon as possible after the meeting; establish a follow-up system to keep projects on track.

Taking Your Group's Temperature

The first twelve chapters provided a framework for making meetings more effective. Groups to which you belong may be already doing many of these things well; perhaps there is only need for a little refinement. Other areas may need more attention. Perhaps most business meetings you attend are effective, but the school board meetings you attend are a disaster.

Awareness is the first step. If you believe there is value in making your meetings more effective using these techniques, share the information with other group members. Please remember that awareness alone will not provide the cure — it takes practice. Start by trying out a few things you think will make a difference. Once your group begins to function more effectively using them, move on to additional things.

What if your group could care less? Is there anything one person can do to make a difference in meetings? Fortunately, the answer is yes. For starters, review the skills for effective participation and facilitation in chapters 5 and 6. Encourage people who bring up ideas; credit them and build ideas to make them stronger. Your example may prompt questions from other group members, and then you can introduce other skills to help your meetings succeed.

When understood and practiced, the steps in this book actually go a lot further than first aid. Many of the techniques provide the antidote to more serious meeting "illnesses" and can also provide remedies for issues that need more intensive care.

Part IV

Beyond First Aid:
Skills for Disruptive Behaviors
and for Specialized Meetings

" Our studies show staff meetings to be 28% more productive
since we got the ejection seat for Mercer."

Beyond First Aid:
Skills for Disruptive Behaviors
and for Specialized Meetings

13. Handling Disruptive Behavior

General guidelines; identifying specific behaviors that disrupt meetings and dealing with them.

14. Electronic Meetings: Telephone and Video Conferences

Tips and techniques for holding meetings when attendees are in different locations.

15. One-on-One Meetings

Manage your time wisely — there's not as much difference as you may think between one-on-one meetings and larger ones.

13

Handling Disruptive Behavior

In this chapter, we will address methods facilitators and group members can use to manage behaviors that throw meetings off-course. It seems that there are always one or more people in meetings who just don't get it. They appear to be interested more in their own agenda than the group's purpose, they choose not to play by the ground rules ... or maybe they just don't know any better. Perhaps they're just having a bad day. Whatever the reasons, a series of disruptions can drag down a meeting quite rapidly. Often, a few "bombs" dramatically change the course of a meeting, sometimes beyond repair. In such cases, more than first aid may be required. It could be time for intensive care.

Addressing these behaviors requires a delicate balance between assertiveness and tact. The goal is to preserve the integrity of the meeting, not to claim a victory over the person or people who are causing the problem. Here are some general guidelines for dealing with behaviors that disrupt meetings:

Focus on the Behavior, Not the Person

It is so tempting to attack the person who seems to be throwing a wrench into anything positive the group is trying to accomplish. After all, they may be attacking others. If we choose this route, however, we may say or do things that we later regret. Worse, attacking people can have longer-term consequences.

> Several years ago, there was a town hall meeting in our community. Several board members prepared general remarks to set the tone of the meeting, including Jay, the mayor. Shortly after Jay began speaking, Sean interrupted him. Sean's voice was loud, and his tone was heated. He attacked the board on everything from policy to minute details of how the library was being run. At first Jay attempted to ignore Sean, which was difficult. Then Jay would say something like, "Sean, hold on a minute," but still Sean kept interrupting.
>
> It quickly turned into a battle of wills, and Jay started talking louder. Sean demanded answers, such as, "What about the cost overruns on the teen center?" and "How come you haven't moved faster on selecting a new waste hauler?" Jay's patience was wearing thin. Finally, he cracked. He turned to Sean and yelled, "Damn it, Sean! Shut up! I've got the floor and I'd like to finish my remarks."

Sean finally sat down after that, and Jay was able to finish. Many people sided with Jay, including me, and said that he was right. However, Jay won the battle and lost the war. Sean was a valuable member of the community, who had been active in many areas. Basically, he had the town's best interests in mind, and he probably didn't know any other way to express his frustrations. After Jay's attack on Sean, he gradually withdrew from participating in most community activities. Nothing Jay said to Sean after that could repair the damage he had done by confronting him.

When one person is embroiled in a battle with another, it is difficult for either of them to rise above the fray. A neutral facilitator can often help, however. Here are some ways a facilitator might handle a disruptive confrontation between two or more people by focusing on the behavior instead of the people:

- Intervene and suggest a process for handling questions and concerns; this takes the burden off the people involved. For example, the facilitator might say something like, "Time out, group. We want to get input from everybody, and we'll make sure there is an opportunity to do that following the board's reports. Make a note of any questions or concerns you have, and we'll address them during the question-and-answer session."

- If tensions and tempers are high, call for a break; approach the people involved privately and ask each person to paraphrase the other's point of view. This will help each to listen, and to see if they really understand each other. If their disagreements are personal or of little interest or don't apply to others, suggest they talk during the break to resolve their differences, perhaps offering to mediate if both agree.

• Addressing the group, explain how shouting and interrupting is not going to accomplish anything. Suggest that each person take five minutes to state his or her point of view, without interruption from the other.

Utilize Ground Rules as a Neutral Judge

Once the group agrees to meeting ground rules, such as "only one meeting/one person talk at a time," the facilitator and others can refer to them when they are violated. While it would be impossible to create a rule in advance for every situation, there are several ground rules that can remind participants in advance of what is expected and can be invoked if necessary. If the behavior continues after a reminder to the group, stronger intervention may be necessary.

Reprimand in Private if Possible

Direct confrontations with people whose behavior is disruptive should be done in private, away from other group members, whenever possible. Staging a public "showdown" may be as disruptive as the original behavior itself and could undermine a facilitator's ability to continue running the meeting.

Of course, it is not always practical to call a break to deal with behaviors that are causing problems. If this is the case, confront the person or people directly in front of other group members. Take a deep breath, and try to remain calm and objective. Focus on concerns such as time constraints, hearing from all group members, and getting ideas expressed before evaluating them.

In private, the conversation can be more candid. Even so, remain calm and explain your point of view directly. The balanced response can be useful in such situations. Start with pluses and move to concerns. For example: "Geraldine, it is obvious you have many ideas to contribute to this brainstorm session. The research you have done gives you a real edge, and we can all benefit from the preparation you have done. However, I need your help. I am concerned that we won't get the best thinking from the rest of the group if they aren't given a chance to contribute their ideas freely. When you interrupt people who are offering their ideas, they tend to close down and keep quiet. How can we get their best thinking and yours as well?" Inviting the person causing the problem to help solve it can be a powerful path to a solution.

Do Not Invite People Who Consistently Cause Problems

Sometimes the subtle approach just doesn't work. If someone consistently disrupts meetings, simply do not invite him/her to the next meeting, and tell the person why. This decision is up to the leader, who is also obliged to tell the person why he/she is not being invited. Of course, if the offending person is the leader or boss, it would be difficult to use this approach. However, an outside facilitator may be able to confront the leader to point out how his/her behavior is affecting the success of meetings.

Specific Disruptive Behaviors

On the following pages are several behaviors which serve no useful purpose in meetings, and possible approaches for dealing with them.

Problem/Behavior	Symptom/Description	Possible Approach
Habitual latecomer	Consistently late to meetings	1) Start on time; after the meeting ask why he/she is always so late. 2) For "first-time offenders," suggest reading the group notes to catch up. 3) Ask him/her to facilitate the next meeting.
Broken record	Repeats points already covered	1) Refer to group notes: "We've covered this, Alan; do you have anything new to add?" 2) Remind of the focus of meeting.
Attention seeking	Talks loudly and often, dominating meeting	1) Move toward the person, then shift focus to someone else. 2) Ask him/her to serve as recorder. 3) Confront directly at break or after.
Horsing around	Clowning, mimicking, disrupting group's work	1) Approach at break and ask him/her to leave if not supportive of the group.

Problem/Behavior	Symptom/Description	Possible Approach
Withdrawal	Drops out from active	Approach and ask his/her opinion on participation in meeting an issue. Be careful not to put the person on the spot: there may be a great idea brewing!
Naysayers	Negates/puts down ideas of others	Enforce ground rule to separate idea generation from evaluation. Introduce "building" language (Chapter 7).
Side conversations	Whispered or louder conversations among two or more members	1) Enforce ground rule of one meeting/one talk at a time. "Hey, folks, let's keep a single focus here." 2) Move closer to persons. Clear your throat. 3) Separate the people. 4) Discuss with people at break.

War stories	Brings up anecdotes that may or may not be related to subject	1) Remind person of the purpose of the meeting and the current focus or topic. 2) Approach person at the break; point out how stories disrupt the group. 3) Use time as a reason to cut stories short.
Time waster	Asks questions that are covered in pre-meeting handout materials	1) Gently remind him/her that the information is in the materials, then move on to someone else.
Competitor	Vying with others to produce the best idea	1) Remind group that idea generating is a team sport, and that all ideas are valid.
Mr./Ms. Minutia	Bring up or dwells on small details not relevant to issue	1) Suggest that the details/issues be set aside "for now," and schedule a time to cover them.
Sidetracker	Brings up side issues not related to current focus	1) Put the issue in the "parking lot" (separate sheet of paper) and cover at end of meeting if time allows.

14

Electronic Meetings: Telephone and Video Conferences

The truth you often hear:

"What's that? Speak up; you're fading in and out."

Thousands of meetings are held every day by telephone. If you include one-on-one phone meetings, the number is in the millions. This chapter will concentrate on techniques for meetings which involve three or more people who are in different locations. Most conference calls are telephone/voice only, although a growing number of conference calls include video transmissions as well.

Telephone Conference Calls

There are many valid reasons to have a conference call meeting. Perhaps the most frequently cited reason is the time and cost savings compared to a live meeting with participants in different locations who must travel to a common location. Telephone conference meetings are also

becoming more common in organizations that have a significant number of telecommuters — people working at home
for all or part of their work. Phone conference meetings can
be highly productive, especially if all the participants have
met each other, and if certain traits of phone conferences are
kept in mind. Here are some techniques and guidelines for
having effective teleconferencing.

- Follow the Four P's of Planning, as you would
  for any meeting: purpose, people, place, and
  preparation. Start by establishing a clear purpose
  for the call: What do we expect to accomplish?
  Also ask: Is this phone meeting really
  necessary?

- Keep the number of participants to a minimum.
  It is often difficult to track who is talking if there
  is a large number of people on the line. It may be
  more productive for the leader to hold a series of
  one-on-one calls, depending on the purpose, or
  if the subject matter is confidential.

- The place may seem inconsequential, but it is
  not. I was a participant in a phone conference
  where one attendee called in from a bank of telephones in an airport. Our meeting was
  constantly interrupted by flight announcements
  and spillover from other phone users. All participants should call in from offices or conference
  rooms that are quiet.

- Preparation is critical. The start time, agenda,
  process, materials, etc., should be planned

thoroughly by the facilitator and communicated to all participants.

- Be sure to communicate exactly how the conferees will join the meeting. Do they call in? Will the originator set things up? Will a telephone operator be involved in connecting? How far in advance of the meeting start time should each party join in?

- An agenda and advance review materials should be prepared and mailed, faxed, or sent by e-mail to every participant in advance of the meeting. The facilitator or leader may want to call key participants to confirm agenda priorities. Send materials no more than a week ahead of the conference; otherwise, they may get lost among other work materials.

- If handouts or other visual aids will be referred to in the phone conference, make sure that they are clearly marked with page numbers and other identification to make them easy to locate and follow. The person referring to the visuals should be clear about which document or visual is being discussed, and confirm that all participants are "on the same page." Example: "We are now going to look at Chart Number Four in Package A, dated June 18."

- Each party should use a high-quality telecommunications system, especially when two or more people are using one phone in a room.

Conference telephones vary widely in quality, and it is wise to invest in a good system if you regularly make conference calls. Some rooms have small microphones suspended from the ceiling through the room, so all conversations can be picked up easily. Additional speakers placed around the room will enable participants to hear other callers better.

- Appoint a facilitator for the phone conference. The facilitator maintains focus by working the agenda, adhering to time frames, and encouraging participation from all group members. The facilitator should go around the conference occasionally to be sure that all points of view are being heard, that people have a chance to participate, and that everyone is still connected.

- When the discussion wanders from the agenda, the facilitator should intervene and suggest handling unrelated issues at a later time. The parking lot technique is useful for such issues.

- Don't discuss documents or other written materials unless all participants have copies.

- Keep in mind that there can be delays in transmission (especially where satellites are involved) that can result in as much as a half-second voice delay. This may not seem long, but it does take some practice to wait a beat after someone finishes before responding. Otherwise, there is a high chance of being cut off. This is a

particular problem with lower-quality conference phones, and conference calls that involve
international parties.

- Participants should interject their speaking with
  frequent pauses, to allow other participants to
  join in with thoughts, ideas and feedback.

- If a conference call has to be rescheduled for
  valid reasons, be appreciative of time zone
  differences and other participants' busy
  schedules.

- Since many voices are similar, each person
  speaking should identify him/herself before
  beginning to speak, throughout the conference.

- All participants should be reminded that extra-
  neous noise such as whispering, paper shuffling,
  chairs moving, etc., are exaggerated in phone
  conferences.

- One person should act as recorder, to capture
  and later summarize key discussion points,
  decisions, action items, and next steps. Because
  other participants will not be able to see the
  group notes, the facilitator or recorder may wish
  to summarize topics as well as progress on the
  agenda "on line" at one or more times during the
  conference.

- If a phone conference is essentially one way, i.e.,
  one person talking and others listening for a
  period of time, the listeners might activate the
  mute button on their phones to minimize noise

on the call. When it is time for feedback, participants can simply deactivate the mute button and begin talking.

- On some conference phone equipment, it is necessary for speakers to directly face the microphone portion of the phone to be clearly heard. If you or your conferees experience cutouts or have other difficulty hearing, one option is to have each participant call in from a separate phone, even from the same office.

- Spend a few minutes debriefing at the end of the meeting, noting what worked and what could be improved.

- The recorder should send the meeting summary, including action steps and responsibilities, promptly to all who participated in the call and to other interested parties.

Video Conference Meetings

Video conferences are growing in popularity, as the cost of equipment and connection time continue to become more affordable. Video and audio connections are also available via the Internet, which opens up many lower-cost possibilities. Most of the suggestions for telephone conference calls apply to video conferences, as well as a few others.

- The time lapse between speaking (and showing) and receiving may be exaggerated in video conferences, depending on the equipment used.

Some transmissions may produce jerky movements that remind you of old movies. This means that anyone speaking should use frequent pauses to make sure that everyone is receiving the communication, and to allow for on-line feedback and discussion.

- Participants should avoid moving around while they are on camera, as rapid movements often become a blur on recipients' screens. Similarly, participants should wear muted clothing — busy patterns and bright colors may also produce blurs.

- Since facilities and transmission times for high-quality video conferences can be very expensive, it is even more critical to adhere to agendas and time schedules. Make sure that any topic discussed on the conference call is applicable to everyone who is connected.

- It is possible to use visual aids on a video conference. They should be big, bold and simple, so participants won't have to squint to figure out what is on them. Better, send hard copies of the visuals by fax or e-mail prior to the conference, so participants can refer to their own copies.

- Although cameras can be adjusted for wide or close-in perspectives, it is important to identify all people who are on-line for the conference, whether they can be seen or not.

- At least one person at each station of a video conference should be thoroughly familiar with the equipment being used, so he/she is able to make adjustments in both audio and video as needed.

15

One-on-One Meetings

The truth you never hear:

"Hi, John. Come on in — you can watch me make important telephone calls while we pretend to have a meeting."

One-on-one meetings cover a wide variety of purposes and styles. They range from informal, impromptu chats to highly structured interviews or performance reviews. Many of the discussions held in the hallway "on the fly" or in our offices do not even count as meetings, in the traditional sense. So why worry about them?

If people allow one-on-one meetings to happen without any ground rules or discipline to keep them on track, they too can become huge time-wasters. Conversely, well-managed one-on-one meetings can accomplish things in a highly effective manner. Since there are only two people involved, such meetings do not have separate facilitators or recorders. Unfortunately, this often leads to the assumption that one-on-one meetings do not need to adhere to techniques that work well in larger group settings. This chapter will address some of the ways to make one-on-one meetings more productive.

- If your time is valuable, set a ground rule that any discussion longer than five minutes must be scheduled in advance, even if it is a one-on-one meeting by telephone. Be careful not to spend more time scheduling your meeting than the meeting itself will take!
- Establish a purpose for every one-on-one meeting. State the purpose at the beginning of the meeting. Example: "I'd like to discuss the latest market research report, and to suggest what action we need to take."
- While your agenda may consist of only one topic, set a beginning and ending time for your meeting.
- Invest in a timing device, such as a miniature hourglass or an electronic timer. When people drop in for an impromptu chat, set the time for five minutes. Unless the meeting has been scheduled for longer, it is over when the alarm sounds, or when the sand runs out.
- If possible, schedule longer one-on-one meetings in some place other than either participant's office. This will ensure that the meeting is not interrupted by telephone calls, and there is

no "home court advantage" because of the subtle trappings and other symbols of an office. The president of one company for which I worked had pewter models of barracudas prominently displayed on his desk. While they did fit his personality, the presence of the barracudas certainly set a tone for any meeting held in his office.

- If you must meet in your or the other person's office, move chairs around so there is not a desk separating you. Hold all telephone calls, sending them to voice mail, or have them screened. If you are expecting an important call, reschedule the meeting. Few things are more frustrating or wasteful than to watch and listen to someone else talking on the telephone.

- Start on time, and regularly monitor the time to make sure you are on track.

- Self-facilitate the meeting to stay focused on the agenda. Defer unrelated items for a later discussion using the "parking lot" technique, or agree to cover them after the primary topic is covered.

- Stop when you have finished the agenda, or when the scheduled time is up, whichever comes first. If you have more to discuss, agree to extend the meeting for a specified period. Always be aware of how you are managing your time!

Appendix

Agendas:

- Sample – Staff Meeting
- Sample – Procedure Review
- Sample – Church Board / Council
- Sample – Board Retreat
- Reproducible Form*

Meeting Effectiveness Checklist:

- Sample
- Reproducible Form*

    * Reproducible forms: Enlarge to 125% to fit on 8-1/2 by 11 paper.

Staff Meeting Notice and Agenda

Group:	HRD - Benefits Section	**Type:**	Staff Meeting
Date:	June 28, 19xx	**Time:**	9:00 - 10:00 a.m.
Place:	Conference Room B		

Leader:	Bob Banks	**Facilitator:**	Michelle Penston
Recorder:	Cynthia Grant	**Timekeeper:**	Jake Edger

Purpose: Regular staff meeting

Participants: Above and Fred Farrel, Doug MacIvers, Lynette Niven, Tondra Staten, Andrew Tsonga

Preparation: Review last minutes; come prepared to discuss new benefits package for manufacturing

Agenda

Item	Person Resp.	Time
Set agenda items	Michelle	9:00 - 9:05
New Manufacturing benefits package	Doug	9:05 - 9:20
#1 agenda items (5 minutes each)	Michelle facilitate	9:20 - 9:45
#2 agenda items (2 minutes each)	All	9:45 - 9:55
Parking lot items	If needed	9:55 - 10:00

Note: The above agenda is useful for a meeting when a single important topic/issue (focus topic) is identified, and when all other agenda items are identified at the beginning of the meeting.

The facilitator lists each #1 and #2 topic on a flip chart pad, then posts it prominently. Note that except for the focus topic, the #1 items are allotted 5 minutes each and the #2 items are allotted 2 minutes each; such times are an arbitrary decision, but should be limited. If there are not enough items to fill the hour, end the meeting early. If there are more than will "fit" into one hour, the facilitator and leader should negotiate with the group to extend the time beyond the hour.

Procedure Review – Meeting Notice and Agenda

Group:	JBA Field Reps	**Type:**	Review/Idea Generation
Date:	July 22, 19xx	**Time:**	9:30 - 11:30 a.m.
Place:	East Conference Room		

Leader:	Amy	**Facilitator:**	Paul
Recorder:	Kevin	**Timekeeper:**	Gretchen

Purpose: Review program procedures, identify issues to resolve; generate ideas; make decisions

Participants: Amy, Kevin, Sarah, Maria, Karen, Gretchen, Chris, Linda, Paul

Preparation: Review original handout/program document; bring specifics from your accounts regarding what's working and what needs improvement

Agenda

Item	Person Resp.	Time
Review initial expectation of program	Amy	9:30 - 9:40
In-depth case: Holmes Brothers	Debbie	9:40 - 9:55
Open discussion: what's working and what needs improvement	All (Paul facilitate)	9:55 - 10:10
Agree on key issues	All (Paul facilitate)	10:10 - 10:20
Idea generation on tip three issues	All	10:20 - 10:40
Break		10:40 - 10:50
Select/develop possible solutions	All (facilitated)	10:50 - 11:10
Determine action steps	Amy	11:10 - 11:20
Parking lot items	All	11:20 - 11:30

Church Board/Council – Meeting Notice and Agenda

Group:	First Church	**Type:**	Monthly council meeting
Date:	September 15, 19xx	**Time:**	Reflection: 10:20 a.m.
Place	Fellowship Hall		Meeting: 10:30 - 11:45

Leader:	Bill	**Facilitator:**	Roberto
Recorder	Flo	**Timekeeper:**	Danny

Purpose: Generate ideas for capital funds drive and update on key events

Participants: Barbara Anderson, Bill Arnold, Marianne Bolton, Tom Fletcher, John Grindela, Danny Morton, Flore Murrow, Sally Taylor, Guest: Ed Hershey

Preparation: Review minutes of last meeting and Ed Hershey's booklet on fundraising. Come with ideas!

Agenda

Item	Person Resp.	Time
Reflection	Bill	10:20 - 10:30
Ideas for capital funds campaign	Roberto facilitate	10:30 - 10:55
Summer youth programs – update	John	10:55 - 11:05
Worship: "Hymn of the Month" program	Sally	11:05 - 11:10
Adult education programs for fall	Jim & Flo	11:10 - 11:20
Interest in starting pastoral care program	Barbara	11:20 - 11:25
Results of New Shepherd program	Marianne	11:25 - 11:35
Senior Minister's report	Bill	11:35 - 11:45
Parking lot items (if needed)	open	

Board Retreat – Meeting Notice and Agenda

Group:	Gizmo Mfg. Assoc.	**Type:**	Board Retreat
Date:	March 9, 19xx	**Time:**	10:30 a.m. - 2:00 p.m.
Place:	Peaceful Resort Conference Center		

Leader:	J. Stenson	**Facilitator:**	C. Hawk
Recorder:	L. Ribern	**Timekeeper:**	G. Ruth

Purpose: Set goals and strategies for coming fiscal year

Participants D. Allen, I. Casey, J. Dibble, R. Kaiser, L. Johnson, L. Ribern, G. Ruth, L. Stensen

Preparation: Current year goals/results for your area or committee; preliminary goals for coming fiscal year

Agenda

Item	Person Resp.	Time
Order lunch, get settled	J. Dibble	10:30 - 10:45
Opening exercise	C. Hawk	10:45 - 11:00
Review last FY goals and results	C. Hawk facilitate	11:00 - 11:20
Next fiscal year goals, future focus	All	11:20 - 11:40
Budget requests	All, I. Casey	11:40 - 12:00
Working lunch; convention program feedback	D. Allen	12:00 - 12:45
Exercise	C. Hawk	12:45 - 1:00
Strategies for achieving goals	All	1:00 - 1:30
New member survey	R. Kaiser	1:30 - 1:40
Parking lot items	C. Hawk facilitate	1:40 - 1:50
Closing exercise	L. Johnson	1:50 - 2:00

Meeting Notice and Agenda

Group: **Type:**
Date: **Time:**
Place:

Leader: **Facilitator:**
Recorder: **Timekeeper:**

Purpose:
Participants
Preparation:

Agenda

Item   **Person Resp.**   **Time**

Meeting Effectiveness Checklist

Group: Benefits Task Force **Date:** 3/14 **Purpose:** New Ideas for benefits

Rate the effectiveness of today's meeting, using a scale of 1 to 5
(1 = great, 5 = lousy)

	Rating	Comments
Overall effectiveness	2	Better than last two sessions
Accomplished our purpose	1	Really productive
Right people in attendance	1	Group has come together
Meeting room worked for our purpose	3	Air conditioning needs fixing!
Participants came prepared to discuss agenda	2	Most read survey and had ideas
Agenda developed and communicated	1	Clear
Meeting stayed on track/focused throughout	3	Wandered off a few times
Presentations well organized and delivered	2	Only one, Jan did her homework
Facilitation effective	3	We are all improving
Used positive feedback methods	3	Need to work on balanced response
Reached consensus	3	Resorted to voting on one issue
We had fun	1	
Action steps assigned	1	Thanks to Sandi volunteering
Started on time	3	Ten minutes late
Ended on time	1	Yes!
What else can we do to improve effectiveness?		Send out review materials *before* each meeting

Meeting Effectiveness Checklist

Group: _____ **Date:** _____ **Purpose:** _____

Rate the effectiveness of today's meeting, using a scale of 1 to 5
(1 = great, 5 = lousy)

	Rating	Comments
Overall effectiveness	____	_____
Accomplished our purpose	____	_____
Right people in attendance	____	_____
Meeting room worked for our purpose	____	_____
Participants came prepared to discuss agenda	____	_____
Agenda developed and communicated	____	_____
Meeting stayed on track/focused throughout	____	_____
Presentations well organized and delivered	____	_____
Facilitation effective	____	_____
Used positive feedback methods	____	_____
Reached consensus	____	_____
We had fun	____	_____
Action steps assigned	____	_____
Started on time	____	_____
Ended on time	____	_____
What else can we do to improve effectiveness?		_____

Charlie Hawkins speaks to organizations about improving their effectiveness through more organized meetings, clear communications and creating a climate for on-going creativity and innovation. He conducts training seminars and in-depth consulting in the areas of communications skills improvement and idea generation. Charlie also facilitates retreats and conferences for organizations of all types.

For further information on Charlie Hawkins' activities and programs, contact:

Seahawk Associates
425 Manzanita Drive
Sedona, Arizona 86336

Phone: 520-204-2511 or 888-285-4295

To order additional copies of

First Aid For Meetings

Book: $14.95   Shipping/Handling $3.50

Contact:

BookPartners, Inc.

P.O. Box 922 • Wilsonville, OR 97070

Fax: 503-682-8684

Phone: 503-382-9821 or 800-895-7323